Indian Low~Fat

COOKING

Indian Low~Fat
COOKING

THE KEY TO A HEALTHY
AND EXOTIC DIET

ROSHI RAZZAQ

THE
APPLE
PRESS

A QUINTET BOOK

Published by The Apple Press
6 Blundell Street
London N7 9BH

ISBN 1-85076-442-5

This book was designed and produced by
Quintet Publishing Limited
6 Blundell Street, London N7 9BH

Creative Director: Richard Dewing
Designer: Chris Dymond
Project Editor: Stefanie Foster
Editor: Michelle Clark
Photographer: Trevor Wood
Home Economist: Judith Kelsey

Dedication
To my mother, Altaf, who constantly tried to share
the secrets of her culinary arts with her daughters,
and was always under the impression that I was not
really listening . . .

Typeset in Great Britain by
Central Southern Typesetters, Eastbourne
Manufactured in Singapore by
J. Film Process Pte Ltd
Printed in Hong Kong by
Leefung-Asco Printers Limited

Contents

Introduction

Image and tradition

I remember reading somewhere that food in most Indian restaurants is so fattening that just by walking past one you are likely to put on weight.

It is not Indian food which is at fault here but the way it is mostly prepared. Indian cuisine is very flexible with the consumption of fat – there are no set rules. There is always room to add, if you like, a bit more, without changing the taste of a curry too much. Some cooks, particularly from

Colourful shrines with offerings are found at every turning in India.

the old school, believe in "the more the merrier" method. The richness of floating fat on top of a serving dish indicates prosperity, generosity and a will to please one's family and friends. So maybe it is this tradition that has contributed a little to the idea that Indian food is fattening.

It must be remembered, too, that ideas about reducing fat in the diet in order for it to be considered healthy are relatively recent. In the times of my mother's generation, things like pure ghee, home-made butter and full-cream milk were considered some of the top health foods and were used quite generously. Vegetable oils were then sneered at and thought of as cheap and nasty products, positively harmful to health.

A change of attitude

Things have changed quite a bit since then. Cooking with vegetable oils is now more than acceptable in the Asian community and the emphasis on pure ghee and home-made butter has become almost a thing of the past. It must be remembered, however, that it is also healthier to use less of *any* fat rather than more.

Nutritional research indicates that it is not carbohydrates but excess fat that must be avoided if we are to be healthy. An awareness of the importance of reducing fat in our diet is gradually affecting what we choose to eat and what we avoid.

Properly prepared Indian food, where care has been taken to keep fat to the minimum, is very healthy and, according to one of the leading food manufacturers in the UK, tops the popularity chart. Also, a great many of the foods that nutritionists highly recommend for healthy living are included in Indian cuisine: pulses and grains, wholemeal flour, natural unsweetened yogurt, garlic, ginger, fresh fruit and vegetables and lean meat or no meat at all. The only dark cloud in an otherwise blue sky is the use of ghee or oils, but, if its use is reduced to the minimum, it will not cause difficulties.

The Taj Mahal, Shah Jehan's mausoleum for his wife Mumtaz Mahal, is synonymous with the romance and grandeur of Indian history.

I know from experience that the natural tendency when cooking a curry is to add (and keep on adding) oil until you have enough in the pan for the onions and spices to cook with great ease. However, all you have to do is resist this inclination and add no more than is absolutely necessary. During the cooking process oil becomes trapped in or hidden by the onions and spices, giving the false impression that there is hardly any, but just carry on cooking over a low heat, stirring from time to time, and be patient – it will make its appearance eventually!

A good thing to do is to keep on decreasing the quantity of oil each time you cook so that you develop an awareness, and the habit, of using only an absolutely essential amount.

Cooking in an excessive amount of oil has just become a habit for most of us. We don't feel comfortable if the onions and spices are not well surrounded by it. It feels as if the presence of oil in quantity is going to make our job easy and, to some extent, it does. As you will have noticed, it certainly prevents the onions sticking to the pan and it also helps to turn them a rich, golden colour in half the time (or so it seems); we feel sure that the little pool of bubbling oil around the masala paste is going to "cook it better" for us! It is this false feeling of comfort and confidence that we must shake off if we are to move in the right direction.

Overcooking vegetables, draining away the goodness and, finally, serving the remains with huge dollops of butter, in an effort to rejuvenate the lifeless vegetables is equally detrimental to healthy eating. Even in these enlightened times, potatoes, if not deep-fried as chips, are roasted in a deep pool of oil to increase their taste and crispiness; sauces and gravies are quite often made from cream, butter and other animal fats; meat still comes with a thick rind of fat. A good curry starts with the leanest meat and the freshest vegetables, so all we have to do is limit the oil we add.

The main thing is that to eat healthily, whatever the cuisine, we have to first have an awareness of *what* we need to eat to be healthy and then work to ensure that we follow the guidelines in the way we *prepare* our food.

Fresh, healthy dishes sold on Indian streets.

The low-fat diet ideal, applied to all the food we eat and to any particular cuisine we choose, offers us great advantages. It ensures good health and we lose excess weight without even trying, which has to be good news!

A 22-week study undertaken at Cornell University, New York found that people lost weight without being on a diet simply by eating low-fat foods. The women who took part in the study followed a diet that provided just 25 per cent of calories from fat, compared to the average contribution of 33 per cent in the American diet. Another interesting finding of the study was that in a traditional slimming diet carbohydrate intake is cut to reduce calories and this slows down the body's metabolism of fats, which is counterproductive. However, low-fat food does not affect the metabolic rate like this. David Levitsky, Professor of Nutrition and Psychology at the University, said, "With low-fat diets, we don't see any metabolism changes. We suspect that metabolism regulatory mechanisms are related to carbohydrate consumption, not fat".

It was found, too, that the women who followed the low-fat diet did not suffer any of the usual side-effects of dieting, like food cravings or depression, that, in the end, make it harder to stick to a diet, especially once they have reached a plateau of weight loss. Professor Levitsky said, "Our studies confirm that people can lose weight without dieting. The weight loss is slow but persistent and should result in a 10 per cent loss of body-weight per year".

The results, published in the May 1991 issue of the *American Journal of Clinical Nutrition*, show that the women who ate low-fat foods lost weight steadily at the rate of about 227g (8oz) a week, even though they were not counting calories or watching the amount of food they were consuming. It is believed that men should respond in the same way, too.

When I first started experimenting with low-fat cooking, I thought that a great deal of taste and flavour would be lost. In order to retain the true essence of Indian dishes, I stuck to the authentic recipe, but simply cut down the amount of fat I used as much as I could. I was delighted with the results – the food tasted, if not better, just as good. An added advantage was knowing that it was healthy to eat this way.

It is true, and I hate to admit it, that frying onions and spices in an adequate amount of oil does enhance the flavour of Indian food and, yes, it does make them easier to cook. However, there are ways to substitute whatever is lacking. Think of the ingredients that will increase the aroma and flavour – a few that come to my mind are ginger, garlic, fresh coriander, roasted cumin and coriander seeds and, of course, my very special recipes for freshly ground garam masala. Slightly increasing the quantities of these herbs and spices and keeping to a good recipe did the trick.

I strongly recommend that you keep a good set of measuring spoons handy and make sure to *always* measure the oil, increasing it only when you have to increase the quantity of food you are preparing because you are feeding more people. Just stick to this rule and you will reap the advantages.

A major part of my work is to pass on this knowledge and an awareness that Indian food can be cooked in a healthy, clean, honest way and still be enjoyed just as much, and that "oily" certainly does not mean "better" or "tastier" as some people tend to believe. Indian food is as popular as ever and we know that it is because it is so delicious, but we also now know that it can be healthy, if only we choose to make it so. Follow my recipes and you will see how.

A few words about Indian ingredients

Read the following sections for the best results when using the recipes in this book and for important information regarding methods and weights and measures. Also, there are some basic recipes here for ease of reference as you will need to refer to them frequently.

MEAT AND POULTRY

Meat, as we know, has a fairly high calorific value, which is mainly due to its saturated fat content. We, therefore, need to take care to choose only the leanest meat and trim away any visible fat before cooking it and, further, eat it in moderation in order to reduce our consumption of fat as much as possible.

Dishes like Bhoona Gosht and the various Kormas where meat is cooked on its own, should always be served with a generous amount of vegetable Bhajis, lentils and grains to balance the meal. The best thing to do is to add a fairly large quantity of vegetables to a small portion of lean meat. This has two advantages: it increases the quantity of the dish without adding very many calories or fat, making it healthy, economical and convenient, as well as adding the flavour of the chosen vegetables. You can create a number of different dishes with their own very distinct flavours just by varying the vegetables slightly. Anyway, in an Indian or Pakistani home, a meat curry is seldom eaten on its own.

SOME USEFUL TIPS FOR MEAT AND POULTRY It has taken me a lifetime of experimentation to find this out, but I now know that the Punjabi way of preparing meat is the best. It is simple and straightforward, easy and economical and, best of all, it is the least fattening.

My mother, being from north India and a city dweller, is proud of the rich and Royal cuisine of that region, which has a strong Moghul influence. She was merely a teenager when, as a young bride, she moved from Lucknow, a most distinguished town, well-known for the sophistication of its Urdu language and its exotic cuisine, to the Punjab. Throughout her married life she has stuck to that particular style of cooking and, in fact, she was somewhat snobbish about the exotic and rich dishes that only she knew how to prepare in that remote village in the Punjab.

When the honeymoon period was over for her and she was allowed to take charge of the kitchen, she found her-self surrounded by the local women, expressing their amazement at her paper-thin chapatis and unique, aromatic dishes cooked in a totally un-Punjabi style. Everyone was extremely impressed and she secretly enjoyed the sense of power it gave her!

Punjabi food is simple and straightforward in comparison. People from that part of India drink a lot of salty Lassi (lightly diluted yogurt drink) and sugarcane juice. Their diet mostly consists of unrefined grains and flours and they eat very little meat.

I knew about the Punjabi method of cooking meat and other dishes all along, but, for some reason, never put it into practice, not until I began searching for ways and means of creating low-fat foods. To my amazement, I realized that the solution had always been there, staring me in the face, and yet I had missed it!

This beautifully prepared meal is typical of food served in thalis.

PUNJABI STYLE OF COOKING MEAT Ordinarily the onions and spices are fried in oil at the initial stage of preparing most meat curries; followed by a sufficient amount of water added to the curry to let the meat cook. In Punjabi cooking, the order is reversed. You begin by adding water into the meat along with onions, ginger, garlic and the rest of the spices and leave it to cook slowly, very much like stew.

The gravy, towards the end of the cooking period, appears to be slightly coated with an oily sheen by the fat released from the meat and bones. So when the time comes to add oil, one tends to use a lot less than otherwise. Best of all, it can be left out altogether in cooking this way, as in some of the recipes such as Daal Gosht and Kadoo Gosht. Each tablespoon of oil costs 120 calories so, if you decide to leave it out, you would be cutting down on calories quite considerably.

Some vegetables, like aubergines, okra, mushrooms and cauliflower, crave for oil and soak it up like a sponge – no matter how much you put in, it keeps on disappearing. You must be firm with yourself when cooking any of these and watch out for the temptation to add "just a bit more".

When buying lamb or beef you will find that either braising steak or meat from the leg or shoulder will be the leanest. Even so, trim any visible fat off before using.

Traditionally, boneless meat is seldom used in Indian cooking. Indeed, bones are included with the meat because they add flavour to the sauce and we all know that the meat nearest the bone is the sweetest.

With mince, to ensure that you are buying the best quality and leanest meat, choose a lean piece of meat yourself and ask the butcher to mince it for you.

The best thing about Indian chicken dishes is that it is never cooked with the skin on. As the skin is where the majority of the fat is, this helps a great deal in our efforts to minimize the presence of saturated fats in our diet.

FISH AND PRAWN DISHES

Apart from the coastal areas in India and Pakistan, eating fish is still not part of the normal diet, and for most people it is something they generally do without.

Yet it is delicious cooked in the Indian style, which is mostly fried, steamed, curried or barbecued. River or freshwater fish is quite sought-after and people travel a great distance to the exclusive places where it can be bought.

When buying fish, make sure that it feels firm and looks plump and not flabby. Pay special attention to the eyes; they must be bright and alert, not dull and cloudy. It is best to buy the fish on the day you intend cooking with it.

Sunset in Cochin – a haven not only for sailors, but also for seafood gourmets.

This colourful display gives an indication of the enormous variety of fresh produce available in India.

VEGETABLES

Back home, the Indian housewife is a bit spoilt when it comes to buying fruit and vegetables. It is generally accepted that it is her right to pick, probe, smell and squeeze any number of fruits and vegetables she likes while selecting the very best ones for her own basket. That's the way my mother shopped, so she was rather shocked when she was not allowed to do so in British markets. However, there are more Asian shops now, where it is understood that the shopper wants to choose the fruit and vegetables bought – and even haggle over the price – and supermarkets have increased their ranges of fruit and vegetables and other ingredients used in Indian cuisine and there, too, you can pick what you want yourself, so things have improved enormously.

My mother's years of experience of examining fruits and vegetables at close range have turned her into an expert buyer. She can sort out the best from the rest at a single glance or by touching them. I have learned a lot from her and pass on some of her best tips here so you know what to look for, too.

SOME USEFUL TIPS FOR CHOOSING VEGETABLES "You have to be extra careful with some vegetables", my mother would say, hoping her grown-up daughters were taking it in. For instance, take okra, the pods should be crisp and fresh enough to snap when you apply just slight pressure. For aubergines she would say that they've "got to be a combination of velvet and marble" – soft and silky to the touch, but, when you tighten your grip a bit, it should feel firm and must spring back immediately no matter how hard the pressure. It must never feel spongy, hollow and dented.

"What about chillies and peppers?" we would ask. "Definitely cool and crisp and shimmering, almost like a mirror, so you can see your reflection in them . . . no good when they are turning red due to staleness and go coarse, wrinkly and limp", she would reply.

For cauliflower she would say, "Well, it should be so tight and firmly held together that even a drop of water would not be able to seep through it! The best ones are like a huge white flower and the green leaves and stalks surround the vegetable like an alert army of guards. It should be cooked unhurriedly, strictly in its own moisture, never

11

Vegetables come just as fresh as you want them.

touch it with water except when you wash it, never. Of course, the cauliflower is at its best when just slightly underdone, every floret separate and firm, ready to be counted. They should be like a superb arrangement of flowers in your serving dish."

DESEEDING GREEN CHILLIES The worst thing about chillies is the fear that they will make a dish too hot. I believe you either use a small amount of green chillies or you don't use them at all. Deseeding them does not make much sense to me: it is a really tedious job and, in my opinion, a waste of time and energy, so I have never understood why all the cookbooks recommend it. The seeds are the hottest part of the chilli, but most recipes call for a small number of chillies or, often, just one. Most Asian households do not remove them and I have certainly never had any complaints from non-Asian friends, so be daring and at least try it and see!

If, after all, you do wish to take the seeds out, cut the chilli open under running water and rinse it out.

When chopping chillies, do not afterwards rub your eyes as they will have some of the oil on them, so wash your hands well after handling chillies.

PULSES

Called daals in India, there are a great many more varieties than the humble red lentil and few beans that have generally been the only ones used in any quantity in the West. With the spread of vegetarianism in more recent years, however, many of them can now be bought from supermarkets, but for an even wider range, try an Indian grocer's. They are available either whole or split, are high in fibre, low in fat

and extremely tasty, so try some of the recipes that use them and reap the benefits.

Channa daal are rather like split peas but are a little bit smaller and a lovely yellow colour.

Chickpeas are readily available either dried or ready-cooked in tins. They are a beige colour, round with a wrinkled appearance. Chickpea flour is used a great deal in Indian cuisine but can be a little difficult to find except in Indian grocer's shops.

Black-eyed beans – called lobia in India – are easier to find now than in the past.

Kidney beans release a toxic substance while they are being cooked, but, as long as you boil them rapidly for at least 10 minutes at the beginning of the cooking time, this substance is destroyed completely.

If you are at all worried, just use the tinned ones, substituting a 395-g (14-oz) tin for every 115 g (4 oz) of dried beans required by the recipe.

Moong daal are the split mung beans that are used to produce bean sprouts.

Split red lentils, or masoor daal in India, are the commonest lentil and can be found everywhere. They are easy to cook and are transformed in Indian dishes into something really special – a far cry from a random addition to a winter stew. The less common whole, unsplit version is also used in Indian cooking.

Garlic – the very soul of almost all Indian dishes.

IN PRAISE OF BASMATI RICE

Nature has blessed basmati rice with the quality of being able to reach its peak of perfection with minimal external help and this puts it in a class of its own. You have to pay a little more for it than other rice, but the end result makes it worth every penny. Not only is it so much easier to cook, its unique taste and flavour add a special touch to the whole meal.

In the West a lot of people still think that the route to perfect rice is one only a few can travel and it definitely isn't them. If you are one of these people, then try basmati rice. Take the example of my daughter. Being an ardent student, she is not too keen on cooking just now, but has good intentions to learn everything properly one day. However, since the age of 12, she has been able to cook rice without any difficulty. If she can do it, anybody can – as long as it is basmati rice, that is.

You will have noticed while washing or rinsing most brands of white rice that the water becomes milky easily. It is this substance that causes all the problems: it thickens into a gluey liquid during cooking, making the rice grains cling together. With basmati rice, on the other hand, the water starts to run clear after the first couple of rinses and, anyway, what milkiness there is is not substantial. This lack of gluten means that the rice grains stay separate, even after they have been thoroughly cooked.

SOME USEFUL TIPS FOR COOKING RICE The two simple secrets of cooking most types of rice are, first, cooking it in exactly the right amount of water and, second, providing the right amounts of heat at the right time.

Measure the cooking water according to the volume of rice to be cooked. Measuring with a tea cup makes this very simple. The rule is, 1½ cups of water for each cup of rice. Remember this simple technique and you won't go wrong. It is as simple as that.

It is a good idea, too, if you have the time, to soak the rice for at least 10–15 minutes in water for the best results.

We have another very useful and clever technique in the East for checking that we have added the right amount of water. Add the water to the rice in a medium-sized saucepan, swirl it around a bit to level the rice, then dip your middle finger into the centre of the pan. For a small quantity of rice, such as is mostly used in this book, the tip of your finger should touch the bottom of the pan and the water level reach the first knuckle of your finger. Add or remove water as necessary. This method never fails and takes only a few seconds to check.

If you are cooking larger quantities of rice, you change the technique slightly: the tip of your middle finger should rest on the surface of the rice, not on the bottom of the pan.

This simple and pretty accurate method has been widely practised in India and Pakistan as long as anyone can remember, passed on from generation to generation.

Another important point to remember is to use a heavy pan with a thick base when cooking rice as a light, thin-based pan will easily burn the rice in the last stage of cooking when almost all the water has been absorbed.

Some basic recipes

CHAPATIS

The chapati is bread at its simplest. The ingredients are just flour and water – no butter, oil or seasoning, not even salt – yet, by bringing these two simple, basic ingredients together, you can create one of the most popular breads eaten in India and Pakistan.

The most common Indian bread – chapati – is simply baked; here, on the inner lining of an oven. Hence the term tandoori roti.

Low-fat chapatis.

There are some Indian dishes that can only be enjoyed with a chapati or some other kind of bread – Cabbage and Carrot Bhaji (see page 64), smoked aubergines and some potato dishes, such as Phalli Aloo (see page 64), Aloo ka Bhurta (see page 70) and other dishes like these that are too dry to serve with rice. Poori, paratha or naan taste very good with these dishes, too. Lightly toasted sliced bread can also be served with most curries or bhajis. Some dry curries and mostly all sorts of bhajis and lentil dishes make excellent toppings for sliced bread, which is often eaten in place of chapatis.

Of all the Indian breads, chapatis contain the fewest calories. Some people like to add a couple of tablespoons of oil to the flour when preparing the dough, but there is no need to do so. It just adds calories unnecessarily.

The best part is that you can make a batch of dough, keep it in the fridge, decide how many calories you can afford to allocate for the bread part of your meal and weigh out an appropriate amount of dough before you cook it (or them). It is easy to work out the calories for the chosen amount of dough – each ounce (25 g) of dough consists of 60 calories. You can see that you are in total control here – your chapatis will have as many calories as you want them to have, no more no less.

Thanks to that wonderful invention, the microwave, a cold, even stale, chapati can be brought back to life within half a minute. Chapatis may also be frozen and rejuvenated by placing them in a microwave for less than a minute.

If heating defrosted chapatis under a grill to reheat them, dampen them slightly and cook them for half a minute on each side. Wrap them in a cloth and use immediately.

Chapati dough can also be frozen and defrosted when required. Otherwise the dough may be kept in the fridge in a covered container for 2–3 days. If you notice that, towards the end of this period, it has gone slightly softer or runny, add a little flour and knead it again for a few minutes to make it as firm and pliable as you like.

It usually takes a little while to get the hang of making good chapatis, but once you master the skill, you will be rewarded with delicious bread in a matter of minutes. Besides, the learning part is such fun, like trying to toss your very first pancake. Naturally, while you are learning to make them, your chapatis will be all sorts of shapes and sizes, but don't be disappointed if some of them come out of the pan looking like Humpty Dumpty with several dangling legs because, no matter how much you go wrong with the shape, they will still taste good.

All you need is a little perseverance and you will soon be creating chapatis with a soft silky texture that are perfectly round.

You will need 175 g (6 oz) of wholemeal flour, 50 g (2 oz) plain flour and 170 ml (6 fl oz) of water.

Total Calories: 800 (including the flour for dredging) – will make 6 chapatis weighing 75 g (3 oz) each, costing 180 calories per chapati.*

*60 calories to 25 g (1 oz) of dough.

Mix a little water at a time into the flour in a mixing bowl. When all the water has been incorporated, start kneading the dough, moistening your hands frequently to ease it off the bowl. Soon it will feel soft and pliable, very much like any other bread dough.

Cover the bowl with a damp cloth and let it stand for at least 30 minutes.

If you think the dough feels too soft and sticky, you can change its texture. Roll the dough onto a floured surface and knead it until it feels firm and is easy to handle – neither wet nor dry (the tendency will be to make the dough firm, but you must remember that if the dough is too firm, the chapatis will turn out crispy and a bit biscuit-like).

Heat a fairly large, thick-bottomed frying pan if you do not have an Indian iron griddle, called a tava, that is used for this purpose. Set it over a fairly high heat to warm it up, then reduce the heat.

Break off a small piece of dough (50–75 g/2–3 oz), roll it into a ball in your palm, then roll it out on a floured surface in the following way. Start rolling it out gently and *lightly* until you have made a thick, round disc. Be really light-handed at this stage as I know from experience that if you press the dough a bit too hard it becomes pasted to the surface. If this does happen, do not worry, just scrape it off completely and start again, remembering to roll it out with feather-light strokes and make sure you keep the weight of the rolling pin itself off the chapati dough, resting it mostly between your fingers and thumbs. You might find it necessary to re-dust the surface several times with flour to stop the dough sticking to it, but be careful not to use more than is really necessary otherwise the dry flour clinging to the chapati will start burning when you cook it, causing the chapati to discolour and a lot of smoke to rise.

Carefully place the rolled out chapati in the hot pan, keeping the heat to medium. You will see that, within a few seconds, a shadowed look will start to spread beneath the chapati. *Immediately* these shadows appear, carefully lift the chapati up by its edge and turn it over. Now watch out for tiny bubbles to form on the surface of the chapati after about 30 seconds. As soon as they appear, lift and turn it over again, for the last time (it is important not to turn the chapati over too many times as it will ruin the texture, making it hard and leathery).

With a clean tea towel, press the chapati down, especially at the edges, to ensure that it cooks evenly. This will make the chapati puff up slightly and golden spots will appear on the surface, indicating that the chapati is cooked (if the heat is right and you get into a rhythm, it should not take more than a minute to cook each chapati). Wrap them up in a tea towel as soon as they are ready, to keep them warm and soft, and eat them straight away as they are at their best when just cooked.

Flour and water being mixed to make chapatis in a family home.

TAMARIND PULP

Tamarind pods are similar in shape and size to a large broad bean, only they are brown in colour, with hard, woody shells around the pulp in the centre. They grow on tall trees and, once peeled, are deseeded and pressed into thick blocks or slabs and dried.

The pulp has a special sour taste that contributes a pleasant tartness to the food or sauces it is added to.

Here is how to make up Tamarind Pulp from dried tamarind.

Break a walnut-sized (about 55 g/2 oz) piece of tamarind from a block of dried tamarind pulp and soak it in 140 ml (5 fl oz) of hot water for an hour or so.

Mash the pulp by rubbing it with your fingers, then push it through a sieve over a bowl and squeeze what remains well to extract the maximum amount of juice from it. Discard the stringy fibrous bits of tamarind that remain in the sieve. The Tamarind Pulp you now have in the bowl will keep in the fridge for a little over a week or you can freeze it in an ice cube tray so that the frozen cubes can easily be added to a dish as and when the recipe calls for it.

TAMARIND SAUCE

The following is a basic Tamarind Sauce recipe, which has an intriguing sweet and sour taste. You can easily turn it into more of a fruit chutney by adding pineapple rings, banana slices and stoned and sliced prunes. Grated carrots can be added too.

It will keep for over a week in the fridge, but if you are making some quite a bit in advance of when you will use it, freeze it in small amounts or ice cube trays.

You will need 140 g (5 oz) of Tamarind Pulp (see the recipe left), ½ teaspoon Roasted and Crushed Cumin Seeds (see page 17), 4–5 teaspoons artificial sugar, a pinch of Garam Masala (see page 18; optional), a pinch of chilli powder, ¼ teaspoon salt and 1 tablespoon of lemon juice.

Dilute the pulp in a saucepan by adding about 120 ml (4 fl oz) of water, then add the Cumin Seeds, sugar, Garam Masala, if using, chilli powder and salt. Bring it to the boil and simmer for a few minutes. Add the lemon juice, then taste the Sauce and adjust the seasoning to your liking. When it is ready, leave it to cool. Serve it chilled.

Tamarind Sauce.

Ginger and Garlic Paste.

GINGER AND GARLIC PASTE

The Ginger and Garlic Paste is very useful and will keep for 2–3 weeks in an airtight jar in the fridge.

It freezes well, too, and there are various ways in which to do this. If you cook Indian food only once in a while, then freezing the Ginger and Garlic Paste in separate, small quantities is the best. Do not keep it in the fridge for longer than 3 weeks or make the mistake of freezing the whole lot in one container. Instead, either freeze it in an ice cube tray reserved for this purpose (as it will impart its flavour to the tray) or spread the paste onto a baking sheet and, once frozen, remove the slab, breaking it into pieces, and keep it wrapped up in a plastic bag.

Alternatively, cut squares of foil and put 2 teaspoonfuls onto each piece and wrap them to make several tiny packets and put these into a plastic container or bag and freeze.

Whichever method you choose, you prepare yourself for months ahead and cooking Indian food becomes so much simpler and you can prepare wonderful dishes whenever you want without having to shop specially, which kills the spontaneity of it all.

Making it is simplicity itself – here is what you do.

You will need 115 g (4 oz) of fresh ginger, lightly scraped, washed and cut into chunks, and the same amount of fresh garlic, peeled.

Put the ingredients into a blender with a very little water, just sufficient to facilitate the grinding process.

Spoon the paste into an airtight jar and store it on the bottom shelf in the fridge or freeze it (see above).

Total cals: 72.

ROASTED AND CRUSHED CUMIN SEEDS

The toasting and crushing of cumin seeds always reminds me of the story of the genie being released from the bottle. The big, bold aroma rushing out of those tiny seeds is just as amazing and powerful to me as the magical genie in the story.

These seeds are termed white cumin seeds and are widely used in Indian cuisine. The seeds are, in fact, brownish in colour, not white at all, but they are known as white cumin to differentiate them from the other variety, black cumin, which is almost black. The term Shahi Zeera is also often used for black cumin. It is important to note that black cumin seeds cannot be substituted for the ordinary white cumin seeds. Also, *never* use horticultural seeds in cooking; always buy them from an Asian grocer's or look in the herbs section of other shops.

For Roasted and Crushed Cumin Seeds you will need 55 g (2 oz) of white cumin seeds.

Heat a heavy frying pan over a medium heat. When it is hot, reduce the heat and drop the cumin seeds into it. Stir them immediately and continuously with a wooden spoon.

In another couple of minutes, the cumin seeds will turn slightly pinkish brown in colour. When they do, switch off the heat, shake and remove the pan from the cooker and leave the seeds to cool.

Once they have cooled, pour them into a blender and grind them for half a second. Alternatively, pour them into a plastic bag and crush them with a rolling pin. The seeds become crispy during the roasting process and so they break easily – only a little pressure is needed to crush them.

Put the Roasted and Crushed Cumin Seeds into an airtight jar immediately and keep it in a cool, dry place.

Roasted and Crushed Cumin Seeds.

ROASTED AND CRUSHED CORIANDER SEEDS

As with cumin seeds, never use horticultural coriander seeds in cooking; always either buy them from Asian grocers or look in the herbs section of other shops.

Coriander seeds can be roasted and crushed in exactly the same way as cumin seeds.

For ground coriander, grind the seeds until they turn into a fine powder. For either kind, storing in an air-tight jar is very important if you are not to lose that delicious nutty aroma.

Garam Masala.

GARAM MASALA

Here is a recipe for a basic garam masala that is invaluable for all kinds of everyday recipes, but you may vary the proportions to satisfy your own tastes once you have tried it.

You will need 55 g (2 oz) black cardamom pods, 25 g (1 oz) piece of cinnamon stick, 25 g (1 oz) of cloves and 55 g (2 oz) of peppercorns.

Heat a large, heavy frying pan and, when it is hot, reduce the heat and add the black cardamom pods and cinnamon stick. With a wooden spoon, move the cardamom and cinnamon around constantly for 2 minutes.

Add the cloves and peppercorns and carry on shuffling the spices around for another 1 minute. Switch off the heat, but still keep on stirring until the pan eventually loses its heat and then leave to cool completely.

Pour the roasted spices into a blender or coffee grinder and grind until you have a fine powder (if the Garam Masala appears coarse and stringy because of the cardamom shells, sieve it and discard what will not pass through the sieve). Store it in an airtight bottle or jar.

GARNISHING GARAM MASALA

Combine 2 tablespoons Roasted and Crushed Cumin Seeds (see page 17) and 2 tablespoons Roasted Coriander Seeds (see above). Grind them for a second in a blender or coffee grinder until you have a fine powder. Add 1 tablespoon of Garam Masala (see above) to it and grind for another second to blend the mixture thoroughly. Store it in an airtight bottle or jar.

GREEN GARLIC SAUCE

Combine in an electric blender 1 small capsicum cut into small pieces, 4 cloves of garlic, 2 whole green chillies (or ¼ tsp chilli powder), 3–4 tbsp lemon juice, 1 tsp sugar, 4 tbsp chopped coriander leaves, ¼–½ tsp salt and 2–3 tbsp water. Chill before using.

DRY WHOLE CHILLIES These are used vastly in Indian cooking and can be used whole or broken or even crushed. It's safer to use them whole, especially if you are not used to very hot food, and you can always discard them just before serving the dish, if you are afraid you might chew on them accidentally. Chilli powder can be substituted, but dry whole chillies have a subtle flavour of their own that you will grow to find indispensable.

Food values

Note that the calories boxes at the end of each recipe give the total calories for that dish and those per portion but do not include those for chapatis or rice or other accompaniments so that you have the flexibility to serve whatever you want with each dish depending on how much of your calorie allowance you have used up.

Dry whole chillies, found in abundance throughout India.

Spicy Meatloaf with Tamarind Sauce

Kofta Sticks

Dahi Channa Chaat

Mixed Vegetable Bhajias

Aloo Ki Tikya

Starters

Fish in Silver Parcels

Crunchy Vegetable Kebabs

Dry Masala Kidney Beans

Spicy Meatloaf with Tamarind Sauce

SERVES 4

INGREDIENTS

100 g/¼ lb onion, roughly chopped
2 tsp grated fresh ginger root
2 green chillies
1 tbsp low-fat natural yogurt
2–3 plump cloves garlic
3 tbsp chopped coriander leaves
225 g/½ lb lean lamb or beef mince
1 tbsp cornflour
½ tsp chilli powder
¼ tsp Garam Masala (see page 18)
small pinch ground mace
2 tsp lemon juice

FOOD VALUE

	TOTAL	PER PORTION (¼)
TOTAL FAT	11.2 g	2.8 g
SATURATED FAT	4.6 g	1.1 g
CHOLESTEROL	135 mg	34 mg
ENERGY (kcals/kj)	447/1883	112/471

This is an excellent party dish because it can be prepared beforehand, chilled a day or two ahead or frozen for a longer period in advance of the party and then simply defrosted and served cold or heated in an oven or microwave on the day. To keep it moist and fragrant, it should be covered with a few fried onions or raw onion rings soaked in lemon juice, sliced tomatoes, fresh mint and coriander leaves. Serve thin slices with onion rings, cucumber and carrot sticks, wedges of lemon and, best of all, Tamarind Sauce (see page 16).

METHOD

1 Put the onion, ginger, green chillies, yogurt, garlic and coriander leaves in an electric blender and blend. Pour the paste into a small bowl.

2 Put the mince into a medium-sized bowl, add the paste together with the remaining ingredients, except the lemon juice.

3 Mix the meat thoroughly, kneading it for a couple of minutes to ensure that the herbs and spices are evenly and well distributed.

4 With moistened hands, press the mixture into a round or oblong loaf shape, ensuring an uncracked, smooth surface.

5 Place the loaf in the middle of a piece of foil large enough to cover it loosely and let it stand for 20–30 minutes before baking and turn the oven on to 425°F/220°C (gas mark 7).

6 Place the wrapped loaf on a baking tray and bake it in the preheated oven for 20 minutes. Unfold the foil to reveal the top of the loaf and bake it for another 5–7 minutes, until it is golden brown.

VARIATION
Kofta Sticks
SERVES 4

Form the mince mixture as for the Spicy Meatloaf into Kofta shapes (small, round balls) and cook them under a hot grill for 7–8 minutes, turning them regularly so that they cook evenly. Drain them on absorbent kitchen paper.

Put the Koftas onto cocktail sticks and serve them on a platter, surrounded by a crispy salad and lemon wedges.

A tablespoon of Green Garlic Sauce (see page 18) mixed into Spring Onion and Cucumber Raita (see page 114) makes a lovely dip for the Koftas and, of course, Tamarind Sauce (see page 16) with grated carrots is an absolute must.

DAHI CHANNA CHAAT
Chickpeas in Yogurt Sauce
SERVES 4

INGREDIENTS

240 ml/½ lb low-fat natural yogurt

75 g/3 oz red and green peppers

75 g/3 oz cucumber, chopped

2 spring onions, chopped

285 g/10 oz chickpeas, tinned, drained

½ tsp chilli powder

1 clove garlic

½ tsp cumin seeds, crushed

1 tsp artificial sugar

salt and pepper to taste

1 tsp dried mint

2 tbsp coriander leaves or fresh mint or chives, chopped

FOOD VALUE

	TOTAL	PER PORTION (¼)
TOTAL FAT	8.6 g	2.2 g
SATURATED FAT	1.7 g	0.4 g
CHOLESTEROL	8 mg	2 mg
ENERGY (kcals/kj)	398/1686	100/422

This dish makes a lovely starter to a summer meal, and it is popular at parties, too. Poured over a jacket potato it makes a substantial meal.

METHOD
1 Whisk 75–90 ml/2½–3 fl oz of water into the yogurt to dilute it.
2 Wash, dry and chop the peppers.
3 Pour the chickpeas into the yogurt. Add the chilli powder, garlic, cumin seeds, sugar and salt and pepper and mix thoroughly. Add the vegetables and mint and mix again. Garnish with chopped coriander, mint or chives and chill well before serving.

Mixed Vegetable Bhajias

SERVES 4

INGREDIENTS

50 g / 2 oz chickpea flour
a pinch of baking powder
¼ tsp chilli powder
a pinch of turmeric
½ tsp cumin seeds, crushed
½ tsp coriander seeds, crushed
1–2 tbsp coriander leaves, chopped (optional)
½ tsp salt
25 g / 1 oz courgettes (zucchini)
25 g / 1 oz aubergines
50 g / 2 oz onion
2 tbsp oil

FOOD VALUE

	TOTAL	PER PORTION (¼)
TOTAL FAT	25.1 g	6.28 g
SATURATED FAT	2.85 g	0.71 g
CHOLESTEROL	0	0
ENERGY (kcals/kj)	388/1614	97/404

What, Bhajias (or Pakoras as they are called in Pakistan) on a low-fat menu? I, too, would have thought it impossible as Bhajias are always deep fried and, as a result, loaded with calories. As they are one of the most delicious savoury snacks in the world, though, I just had to work out a receipe for Bhajias that would be suitably low in fat and I have done it. They are not as crispy and light in texture as they would have been had they been deep-fried, but, even so, the combination of these spicy Bhajias and tangy Tamarind Sauce (see page 16) still tastes heavenly and can be eaten with a clear conscience.

I use chickpea flour (basen) for the batter but you can also try cornflour, but the results will not be quite as good.

METHOD

1 Sift the chickpea flour and baking powder into a small mixing bowl. Add the chilli powder, turmeric, cumin and coriander seeds, coriander leaves, if using, and salt. Add about 75 ml/2½ fl oz of water and mix it well, making a smooth batter. Let it stand for 15 minutes.

2 Wash, dry and slice the courgettes and aubergines finely. Slice the onion finely, too. Just before you are ready to cook, add these vegetables to the chickpea batter, coating them well.

3 Heat half the oil in a medium-sized non-stick frying pan, then spoon the battered vegetables into it. Reduce the heat to medium and cook for about a minute. Turn them over and cook for another minute or so, shaking the pan frequently.

5 Try to get them as crispy as you possibly can in that limited amount of oil. Remove and drain on absorbent paper. Repeat using the second tablespoon of oil and serve these hot.

ALOO KI TIKYA
Spicy Potato Patties
SERVES 4

INGREDIENTS

400 g/14 oz potatoes
1 tbsp lemon juice
1 tbsp fresh mint, chopped, or unsweetened mint sauce
½ tsp salt
1 small onion, finely chopped
2 tsp coriander seeds, crushed
1 tsp cumin seeds
¼ tsp chilli powder
2 green chillies, finely chopped
3 tbsp coriander leaves, chopped
1 size 4 egg
2 tsp oil

FOOD VALUE

	TOTAL	PER PORTION (¼)
TOTAL FAT	11.7 g	2.9 g
SATURATED FAT	2.2 g	0.6 g
CHOLESTEROL	181 mg	45 mg
ENERGY (kcals/kj)	438/1646	110/412

Potatoes have a natural affinity with the herbs and spices and are especially receptive to the cumin, fresh coriander and green chilli of this recipe.

The Tikyas (burgers) freeze well and so they can be microwaved whenever needed. They go well with Tamarind Sauce (see page 16).

METHOD

1 Peel and chop the potatoes and boil them until they are tender.

2 Meanwhile, mix the lemon juice, mint or mint sauce and a pinch of salt into the onion. Set this mixture for filling the patties to one side.

3 Break the potatoes and mash them lightly so the mixture is still slightly lumpy. Add the coriander and cumin seeds, chilli powder, green chillies, coriander leaves and salt. Blend these herbs and spices well into the mashed potatoes.

4 Divide the potato mixture into 8 equal portions. Dampen your hands a little and roll each portion in your palm. Make a dent in the ball you've made, fill it with a tiny amount of the mint and onion filling, cover the filling and flatten each ball gently to form a burger shape.

5 Just before frying these patties, whisk the egg and season it lightly. Heat a large, non-stick frying pan and grease it with half the oil. When the pan is fairly hot, dip each potato Tikya into the egg and put it in the pan. Put the first 4 Tikyas in the pan to sizzle for a minute or so, then turn them over and cook the other side until they are crispy and golden brown. Cook the remaining 4 Tikyas in the same way.

Fish in Silver Parcels

SERVES 1

INGREDIENTS

125 g/5 oz cod, coley or haddock fillet
2 tsp lemon juice
salt to taste
1 tbsp coriander leaves
1 fat clove garlic
1 green chilli
1 tsp desiccated coconut
¼ tsp sugar
2 tsp low-fat natural yogurt

FOOD VALUE

	TOTAL	PER PORTION
TOTAL FAT		4.1 g
SATURATED FAT		2.9 g
CHOLESTEROL		59 mg
ENERGY (kcals/kj)		137/579

The inspiration for this recipe is a well-known, festive Parsee dish known as Patra ni Macchi. The word "patra" means leaf and is used here because the fish pieces are first marinated, then wrapped in banana leaves before steaming, which results in fish that is moist and succulent.

The original recipe includes a very generous quantity of fresh coconut, which is unfortunate as the calories contained in that one ingredient are greater than the rest of the meal! Without it, though, this dish is very low in calories. Still, perhaps you could add just a hint of the traditional nutty flavour by adding a small quantity in the green masala paste rather than leave it out completely.

METHOD

1 Marinate the fish in the lemon juice and season lightly. Leave it to marinate for 15–20 minutes.

2 Grind the coriander leaves, garlic, chilli and coconut in a blender until the mixture forms a paste, then add the sugar, yogurt and a pinch of salt, and mix them in thoroughly.

3 Smother the fish with this green masala paste on both sides. Wrap the fish loosely in foil and leave it to marinate for at least an hour in the fridge. During that time, preheat the oven to 400°F/200°C (gas mark 6).

4 Place the foil parcel on a baking tray and bake it in the preheated oven for about 15 minutes, or until it is just cooked through. Serve with a salad, and Tamarind Sauce (see page 16).

Crunchy Vegetable Kebabs

SERVES 4

INGREDIENTS

| 175 g/6 oz cauliflower |
| 75 g/3 oz cabbage |
| 75 g/3 oz carrots |
| 50 g/2 oz spring onions or onion |
| 175 g/6 oz potatoes, boiled |
| 15 g/½ oz sunflower seeds |
| 1 green chilli, chopped |
| 2–3 cloves garlic, chopped |
| 1 tsp ginger, grated |
| ½ tsp chilli powder |
| ½–1 tsp salt |
| ½ tsp cumin seeds, crushed |
| freshly ground black pepper to taste |
| 3 tbsp coriander leaves, chopped |
| 1 tbsp lemon juice |
| 1 tbsp oil |
| 1 size 4 egg, beaten |

FOOD VALUE

	TOTAL	PER PORTION (⅛)
TOTAL FAT	25.7 g	3.2 g
SATURATED FAT	4.1 g	0.5 g
CHOLESTEROL	181 mg	23 mg
ENERGY (kcals/kj)	496/2071	62/259

Kebabs in Indian cooking are burger shapes with or without a filling rather than chunks of meat, fish or vegetables strung on sticks and grilled. Spicy and delicious, they are very good to have in the freezer for snacks, starters or main meals.

These crunchy Kebabs, together with Tamarind Sauce (see page 16) and Green Garlic Sauce (see page 18) taste like a "piece of heaven", as my daughter would put it!

METHOD

1 Grate the cauliflower, cabbage and carrots.

2 Chop the onions quite finely.

3 Mash the potatoes.

4 Toast the sunflower seeds, then set them to one side.

5 Combine the grated vegetables with the spring onions or onion, mashed potatoes, green chilli, garlic and ginger.

6 Add the chilli powder, salt, cumin seeds, freshly ground black pepper, coriander leaves and lemon juice. Mix the herbs, spices and vegetables together thoroughly. Then mix in the sunflower seeds.

7 Divide the mixture into 8 equal portions and make burger shapes. Keep the Kebabs in the fridge for an hour or so to firm up.

8 Grease a large, non-stick frying-pan with half the oil. Dip the first 4 Kebabs into the egg and fry them gently over a medium heat. Turn them once, cooking both sides until they are crispy and golden brown. Use the remaining oil to cook the second batch of Kebabs.

Gathering in the nets on Kovalam beach. The simple restaurants along what is often called India's finest beach offer a range of excellent seafood.

MASALA RAJMA
Dry Masala Kidney Beans
SERVES 4

See the information about cooking kidney beans on page 12 before starting this recipe.

INGREDIENTS

125 g/5 oz red kidney beans, dried

2 tsp Ginger and Garlic Paste (see page 17)

1 green chilli, chopped

½ tsp chilli powder

½ tsp salt

¼ tsp turmeric

¼ tsp Garam Masala (see page 18)

¼ tsp cumin seeds, crushed

2 tbsp coriander or mint leaves, finely chopped

1 tbsp lemon juice

FOOD VALUE

	TOTAL	PER PORTION (¼)
TOTAL FAT	1.8 g	0.5 g
SATURATED FAT	0.25 g	0.06 g
CHOLESTEROL	0	0
ENERGY (kcals/kj)	266/1416	66/354

Red kidney beans are here cooked with spices until all the moisture has evaporated away and they are soft, and filled with aromatic juices.

You can substitute them for calorie-laden roasted peanuts at parties or a handful of these scattered over a crispy salad, not only adds to the colour, but also provides a tasty, nutritious meal. Add them to any of the raitas and these pretty red beans, almost drowning in a pool of cool yogurt, make an easy meal that is a very enjoyable change.

METHOD

1 Soak the kidney beans for 3–4 hours in a medium-sized heavy saucepan. Drain them well, then pour in 570 ml/1 pint of water.

2 Add all the ingredients except the coriander or mint leaves, cumin seeds and lemon juice. Cook over a high heat for the first 25–30 minutes, then reduce the heat and simmer for the next 35–40 minutes, reduce the heat and simmer for the next 35–40 minutes or until the beans are tender but not broken or mushy.

3 Remove the lid and cook until all the moisture evaporates and the beans are soft but dry, taking care to ensure that they do not burn or stick to the pan.

4 Mix in the cumin seeds, coriander or mint leaves and lemon juice. Shake the beans, when they have cooled, remove them to a serving platter.

Meat Dishes

BHOONA GOSHT
A Semi-dry Lamb or Beef Curry with Peppers
SERVES 4

INGREDIENTS

350 g/¾ lb leg of lamb, boned

50 g/2 oz green pepper

75 g/3 oz onion, chopped

1 tbsp Ginger and Garlic Paste
(see page 17)

½ tsp chilli powder

¼ tsp turmeric

½ tsp Garam Masala (see page 18)

½–¾ tsp salt

2 tbsp oil

75 g/3 oz tomatoes, chopped

chopped chives or spring onions,
to garnish

FOOD VALUE

	TOTAL	PER PORTION (¼)
TOTAL FAT	53.4 g	13.3 g
SATURATED FAT	17.4 g	4.4 g
CHOLESTEROL	277 mg	69 mg
ENERGY (kcals/kj)	812/3390	203/848

METHOD

1 Wash and cut the meat into 2.5-cm/1-inch cubes.

2 Cut the green pepper into 1-cm/½-inch squares.

3 Put the meat in a medium-sized heavy saucepan. Add the onion, Ginger and Garlic Paste, chilli powder and turmeric, Garam Masala and salt. Pour in 275 ml/10 fl oz water, stir then cover the pan and bring it to the boil. Reduce the heat and simmer for 30–35 minutes.

4 Remove the lid, turn up the heat and stir continuously until the moisture evaporates and the masala paste thickens. Then add the oil, stir it in and cook for another minute or so. This is a crucial time for the dish: the spices and oil must marry up well with the meat. Fry the mixture, adding a tiny amount of water, until the masala paste turns a slightly darker shade and begins to appear slightly glazed (this will take a couple of minutes).

5 Add the pepper and tomato, mix in well and cook briefly (2–3 minutes).

6 Let the Bhoona Gosht stand for 3–4 minutes before serving, then garnish the dish with the chives or spring onions.

KADOO GOSHT
Lamb with Chunks of Marrow
SERVES 4

INGREDIENTS

350 g/¾ lb leg of lamb, boned

350 g/¾ lb marrow

½–¾ tsp chilli powder

¼ tsp turmeric

½ tsp Garam Masala (see page 18)

½ tsp ground coriander

1 tsp salt (optional)

2 tbsp oil

75 g (3 oz) chopped onions

1 tbsp Ginger & Garlic Paste (see page 17)

100 g/¼ lb tomatoes, chopped

1 green chilli, chopped

¼ cup coriander leaves, chopped

FOOD VALUE

	TOTAL	PER PORTION (¼)
TOTAL FAT	53.9 g	13.5 g
SATURATED FAT	17.4 g	4.4 g
CHOLESTEROL	277 mg	69 mg
ENERGY (kcals/kj)	842/3516	210/879

This is light, summer curry. You might think a *summer* curry is odd, but the cool, clear-tasting marrow does remind me of hot, summer days, and is delicious served on a mound of piping hot basmati rice.

You can use either braising steak or leg of lamb for this dish. Cook a little longer if you are using tougher cuts.

METHOD

1 Wash and cut the meat into 2.5-cm/1-inch cubes.

2 Peel the marrow, just taking off the skin and the minimum of flesh, and cut it into approximately 2.5-cm/1-inch cubes.

3 Put the meat into a heavy saucepan, add 275 ml/10 fl oz of water and the chilli powder, turmeric, Garam Masala, coriander, if using, and salt along with the chopped onions and Ginger and Garlic Paste. Bring to the boil, reduce heat, cover and simmer for 35–40 minutes.

4 Lift off the lid, turn up the heat and stir continuously until the moisture has evaporated and the curry thickened a bit. Then add the oil and fry the spices well. Lower the heat and cook this mixture for 2–3 minutes, adding a small quantity of water whenever needed until the spices darken and glaze slightly.

5 Stir in the marrow chunks and tomato. Add 275 ml/10 fl oz of water, cover the pan and cook for 10–12 minutes over a low heat. Add the green chilli and half the coriander leaves. Stir and cook for 2–3 minutes. Remove the pan from the heat, add the remaining coriander leaves and let the dish stand for 3–4 minutes before serving.

GAJER GOSHT
Beef with Carrots and Peppers
SERVES 4

INGREDIENTS

350 g/¾ lb beef braising steak
225 g/½ lb carrots
¾ tsp chilli powder
¼ tsp turmeric
½ tsp Garam Masala (see page 18)
1 tsp salt
75 g/3 oz tomatoes, chopped
2 tbsp oil
1 tbsp low-fat natural yogurt
50 g/2 oz green pepper, sliced
1 green chilli, chopped
½ tsp sugar
1 tbsp Ginger & Garlic Paste (see page 17)
2 cloves garlic, chopped or crushed
1 tbsp mint leaves, to garnish

FOOD VALUE

	TOTAL	PER PORTION (¼)
TOTAL FAT	50 g	12.5 g
SATURATED FAT	14.5 g	3.6 g
CHOLESTEROL	158 mg	40 mg
ENERGY (kcals/kj)	791/3295	198/824

This seemingly ordinary dish has a quite unusual, surprisingly delicious taste. The tomatoes and natural yogurt make it wonderfully tangy and it is a very convenient dish to make the year round because of the choice of the vegetables.

METHOD

1 Cut the beef into 2.5-cm/1-inch cubes.

2 Scrape, wash and cut the carrots into tiny quarters by slicing the carrot lengthwise into 4 strips and then slicing across while holding the strips together.

3 Put the meat into a heavy saucepan, add 275 ml/10 fl oz of water, onions, Ginger and Garlic Paste and the chilli powder, turmeric, Garam Masala and salt. Bring it to the boil, then reduce the heat, cover and simmer for 35–40 minutes.

4 Now add the carrots, tomatoes and yogurt, stirring them in well. Cover and cook for 8–10 minutes over a low heat. Then add the pepper, green chilli, sugar and chopped garlic. Stir to mix them in well. Cook for another 4–5 minutes. Remove the pan from the heat and serve, garnished with the mint leaves.

DAAL GOSHT
Lamb with Lentils
SERVES 4

INGREDIENTS

285 g/10 oz shoulder of lamb
100 g/¼ lb red lentils
75 g/3 oz onion, chopped
1 tbsp Ginger and Garlic Paste (see page 17)
1 tsp chilli powder
¼ tsp turmeric
½ tsp Garam Masala (see page 18)
1 tsp salt
1–2 green chillies, chopped
½ tsp cumin seeds, crushed
2 tbsp coriander leaves, chopped

FOOD VALUE

	TOTAL	PER PORTION (¼)
TOTAL FAT	25.7 g	6.4 g
SATURATED FAT	11.8 g	3 g
CHOLESTEROL	217 mg	54 mg
ENERGY (kcals/kj)	790/3333	198/833

A family favourite all the year round, you can use channa, maash, moong, masoor or whatever type of lentil you happen to have. They each have a distinctive taste and flavour of their own so whenever you use a different one, you are creating a new dish with a special taste of its own. Here I am using masoor daal, or red lentil. It is easily available everywhere and this particular type of lentil does not need presoaking.

The remarkable thing about this recipe is that no oil is used, which makes it especially low in fat.

METHOD
1 Wash and cut the meat into 2.5-cm/1-inch cubes.

2 Wash and drain the lentils then put them into a small bowl and keep them to one side.

3 Put the meat in a heavy saucepan, together with the onion, Ginger and Garlic Paste, chilli powder, turmeric and salt. Pour in 240 ml/8 fl oz of water, bring it to the boil, then reduce the heat and cook for 20–25 minutes.

4 Now increase the heat and stir continuously until most of the moisture has evaporated.

5 Add the lentils, together with 425 ml/¾ pint of water and leave them to cook over a low heat for 30–35 minutes. Mix well with a wooden spoon during this time until they are thoroughly dissolved into the mixture and begin to look quite "mushy".

6 Add the Garam Masala, green chillies and the cumin seeds, then simmer gently for another 3–4 minutes.

7 Add most of the coriander leaves and stir to mix them in. Garnish with the reserved few leaves.

BHINDI GOSHT
Lamb with Okra and Onions
SERVES 4

INGREDIENTS

350 g/¾ lb lean shoulder of lamb

225 g/½ lb okra (prepared weight)

1 tsp chilli powder

¼ tsp turmeric

½ tsp Garam Masala (see page 18)

1 tsp salt

*1 tbsp Ginger and Garlic Paste
(see page 17)*

175 g/6 oz onion, sliced or chopped

2 tbsp oil

100 g/¼ lb tomatoes, chopped

½ tsp cumin seeds, crushed

a pinch of freshly ground black pepper

2 tsp lemon juice

FOOD VALUE

	TOTAL	PER PORTION (¼)
TOTAL FAT	55.8 g	13.9 g
SATURATED FAT	18.1 g	4.5 g
CHOLESTEROL	277 mg	69 mg
ENERGY (kcals/kj)	906/3782	227/946

METHOD

1 Wash and cut the meat into 2.5-cm/1-inch cubes.

2 Wash the okra and dry it well (it is important to remove as much water as possible). Trim the ends off and cut them into 2 or 3 pieces.

3 Put the meat into a medium-sized heavy saucepan, add 275 ml/10 fl oz of water and the chilli powder, turmeric, Garam Masala, salt and Ginger and Garlic Paste. Add, too, a third of the onion, reserving the rest for a later stage. Bring the mixture to the boil, then reduce the heat, cover and simmer for 25–30 minutes.

4 Be extra attentive during this stage as it is the most critical point in the cooking process. Remove the lid, then add the oil and stir continuously over a high heat until the liquid thickens to a paste, darkens a bit and tiny wells of oil begin to appear, which will take 2–3 minutes. Keep adding a little water from time to time so that the mixture cooks without sticking.

5 Stir in the okra, chopped green chilli, tomatoes and remaining onion. Cover and cook for 20–25 minutes over a low heat. You will find that the okra will release a sort of gummy substance, but it will soon be absorbed. Stir the mixture once lightly during this time. Lastly, sprinkle the cumin seeds, a grinding of black pepper and the lemon juice over the top, then let it stand for a few minutes before serving.

A view from Agra's fort – Shah Jehan's palace and later his prison. The solace of his captivity was a distant view of the Taj.

BANGON GOSHT
Lamb with Aubergines
SERVES 4

INGREDIENTS

350 g/¾ lb leg of lamb
350 g/¾ lb aubergines
1 tsp chilli powder
¼ tsp turmeric
½ tsp Garam Masala (see page 18)
1 tsp salt
100 g/¼ lb onion, chopped
2 tbsp oil
1 tbsp Ginger and Garlic Paste (see page 17)
1–2 green chillies
75 g/3 oz tomatoes, chopped
1 tbsp low-fat natural yogurt
1 tbsp Tamarind Pulp (see page 16), (optional) or 2 tsp lemon juice
4–5 curry leaves (optional)
½ tsp sugar
½ tsp cumin seeds, crushed
2 cloves garlic, crushed
any green leaves (mint, coriander, chives or spring onion), to garnish

FOOD VALUE

	TOTAL	PER PORTION (¼)
TOTAL FAT	55 g	13.8 g
SATURATED FAT	18 g	4.5 g
CHOLESTEROL	277 mg	69 mg
ENERGY (kcals/kj)	903/3769	226/942

Traditionally, any remaining onions are fried before being added to the dish in the last stage of cooking, but we shall, of course, not do such a wicked thing!

METHOD

1 Wash and cut the lamb into 2.5-cm/1-inch pieces.

2 Wash, dry and slice the aubergines into quarters lengthwise, then, holding the strips together, cut them across into 2.5-cm/1-inch chunks. Put the aubergine into a colander, sprinkle it generously with salt and leave it to stand for 40–50 minutes until the bitter juices have run out. Rinse it under cold water, drain and put to one side.

3 Put the meat into a medium-sized heavy saucepan, add 275 ml/10 fl oz of water, the chilli powder, turmeric, Ginger and Garlic Paste, Garam Masala and salt and half the onions, reserving the rest for later. Bring the mixture to the boil, then reduce the heat, cover and simmer for 25–30 minutes.

4 Be careful at this stage as it is crucial to the success of the dish. Remove the lid, add the oil and stir continuously over a high heat until the liquid thickens to a paste, darkens a little and tiny wells of oil appear, which takes about 2–3 minutes. Add a little water from time to time to ensure that the mixture cooks without sticking.

5 Now add the aubergine, tomato, remaining onions and yogurt. Mix them in well and let the mixture cook gently for a further 25–30 minutes, stirring occasionally during this time.

6 Add the Tamarind Pulp or lemon juice and curry leaves, if using. Also stir in the sugar, cumin seeds and crushed garlic, then simmer for another 10–12 minutes. Garnish the dish with your chosen green leaves.

KEEMA MUTTER
Mince with Peas and Peppers
SERVES 4

INGREDIENTS

350 g/¾ lb beef or lamb mince

100 g/¼ lb onion, sliced or chopped

100 g/¼ lb tomatoes, chopped

1 tbsp Ginger and Garlic Paste
(see page 17)

½–1 tsp chilli powder

¼ tsp turmeric

½ tsp cumin seeds

½ tsp Garam Masala (see page 18)

1 tsp salt

125 g/5 oz peas, fresh or frozen

1 green chilli

2 tbsp coriander leaves or spring onions,
chopped

FOOD VALUE

	TOTAL	PER PORTION (¼)
TOTAL FAT	18.5 g	4.6 g
SATURATED FAT	7.2 g	1.8 g
CHOLESTEROL	207 mg	52 mg
ENERGY (kcals/kj)	587/2463	147/616

Keema Mutter is a quick, easy and versatile everyday dish. It is always handy to have in the fridge, too, for lovely snack meals or to fill sandwiches. You will notice that no oil has been used in this dish!

METHOD

1 Put the mince into a medium-sized heavy saucepan together with the onion, tomato, Ginger and Garlic Paste and chilli powder, turmeric, cumin seeds, Garam Masala and salt. Mix them well, cover the pan and cook for 25–30 minutes over a low heat, stirring it occasionally during this time to make sure it does not catch.

2 Remove the lid and stir over a high heat to evaporate the excess liquid. Then add the peas and green chilli. Cover and cook for a further 5–7 minutes.

3 Add half the coriander leaves or spring onion and cook for 2–3 more minutes. Remove the pan from the heat and garnish with the remaining coriander or spring onion.

KEEMA GOBHI
Mince with Cauliflower
SERVES 4

INGREDIENTS

1 tbsp oil
3–4 whole dried chillies or 1 tsp chilli powder
½ tsp cumin seeds
285 g/10 oz lean lamb or beef mince
75 g/3 oz onion, chopped
¼ tsp turmeric
½ tsp Garam Masala (see page 18)
1 tsp salt
350 g/¾ lb cauliflower florets
75 g/3 oz tomatoes, chopped
1 tbsp ginger, grated
3–4 fat cloves garlic, crushed or chopped
2–3 tbsp coriander leaves (optional)

FOOD VALUE

	TOTAL	PER PORTION (¼)
TOTAL FAT	27.3 g	6.8 g
SATURATED FAT	7.3 g	1.8 g
CHOLESTEROL	162 mg	40.5 mg
ENERGY (kcals/kj)	596/2493	149/623

METHOD

1 Heat the oil in a medium-sized heavy saucepan. Add the dried chillies (do not put the chilli powder in at this stage if you are using it instead) and cumin seeds. Fry these for half a minute over a medium heat, then add the mince and onions, stirring continuously.

2 Add the chilli powder now, if using, the turmeric, Garam Masala and salt and mix thoroughly. Cover the pan, lower the heat and simmer for 20–25 minutes.

3 Add the cauliflower, tomatoes, ginger, garlic and the green chillies. Cook without a lid over a medium heat for 10–12 minutes. Once the moisture has evaporated, stir in the coriander leaves, reserving some for garnishing.

DO PIAZA
Lamb with Twice the Amount of Onions
SERVES 4

INGREDIENTS

350 g/¾ lb shoulder of lamb
3–4 whole dried chillies
1-cm/½-inch piece cinnamon stick
3–4 whole cloves
2 black cardamom pods, bruised (optional)
½ tsp peppercorns (optional)
1 tsp cumin seeds
400 g/14 oz onions, sliced
100 g/¼ lb tomatoes, chopped
1 tsp salt
2 tbsp oil
1 tbsp Ginger and Garlic Paste (see page 17)
2 green chillies, chopped

FOOD VALUE

	TOTAL	PER PORTION (¼)
TOTAL FAT	53.9 g	13.5 g
SATURATED FAT	17.4 g	4.4 g
CHOLESTEROL	277 mg	69 mg
ENERGY (kcals/kj)	926/3863	232/966

This north-Indian dish has a unique taste and flavour all its own. The only thing is chopping up all those onions, but a well-made Do Piaza is an experience worth every tear!

A tip for lessening the effect of the onions is to leave them in the fridge for a couple of days before using.

METHOD

1 Wash and cut the lamb into 2.5 cm/1-inch chunks.

2 Put the meat into a heavy saucepan that has been greased with 1 tbsp oil. Sprinkle all the whole spices over it, then the onions and tomatoes. Sprinkle the salt over, cover and leave it to simmer gently for 30 minutes.

3 Give it a good stir now, then add the remaining oil, Ginger and Garlic Paste and green chillies. Cook it, uncovered, for another 15 minutes or until the moisture almost disappears.

4 Increase the heat and stir continuously so that the onions become pulpy and the mixture takes on a slightly glazed look. Pick out the whole spices before serving, if preferred.

Mince with Cauliflower.

KOFTA CURRY
Meatballs in Thick Gravy
SERVES 4

INGREDIENTS

KOFTAS

1 tbsp chickpea flour, roasted, or cornflour
75 g/3 oz onions, chopped
2 tsp grated ginger
3 fat garlic cloves
½ tsp chilli powder
¼ tsp Garam Masala (see page 18)
½ tsp salt
3 tbsp coriander leaves
1 green chilli, finely chopped
350 g/¾ lb lean lamb or beef mince

SAUCE

2 tbsp oil
75 g/3 oz onion, finely chopped
¼ tsp cumin seeds
2–3 green cardamoms
2 tsp Ginger and Garlic Paste (see page 17)
½ tsp chilli powder
¼ tsp turmeric
¼ tsp Garam Masala (see page 18)
¾ tsp salt
75 g/3 oz tomatoes, chopped
1 green chilli, chopped
½ tbsp low-fat natural yogurt
2 tbsp coriander leaves, chopped

FOOD VALUE

	TOTAL	PER PORTION (¼)
TOTAL FAT	53.8 g	13.5 g
SATURATED FAT	17.5 g	4.4 g
CHOLESTEROL	277 mg	69 mg
ENERGY (kcals/kj)	952/3982	238/996

Eastern herbs and spices work their magic best of all when the meat or poultry you want to use in a dish is marinated in them. In this recipe, the humble meatball is turned into something really special.

In the original recipe, roasted chickpea flour and ground poppy seeds are used to bind and improve the texture of the meat, but, in my experience, using cornflour instead of poppy seeds is simple and almost as effective.

METHOD

1 First make the Koftas. If using chickpea flour, dry roast it in a heavy frying pan, using a wooden spoon to move the flour around continuously until it changes to a slightly darker shade (2–3 minutes). Let it cool.

2 Grind the onion, ginger, garlic, coriander leaves and green chilli in a blender.

3 Put the mince into a bowl and add all the above ingredients into it including the chilli powder, Garam Masala, salt and chickpea flour or the cornflour. Knead to mix them

together thoroughly. Set the mixture to one side for 10–15 minutes for the spices to mingle.

4 Divide the mixture into 16 equal portions and, moistening the palm of your hand, roll each portion into a smooth round ball. Cook the Koftas under a hot grill for 10 minutes (turning them once) to drain off all the excess oil.

5 Now, make the sauce. Heat the oil in a medium-sized, heavy saucepan. Add the onion and fry gently. Add the cumin seeds and cardamom pods. When the onion is deep, golden brown, add the Ginger and Garlic Paste, remaining spices and salt. Cook this masala paste well, adding a little water when necessary, until the spices darken a little and tiny wells of oil appear on the surface of the mixture.

6 Add the tomatoes and yogurt and stir continuously.

7 Reduce the heat a little and drop the grilled Koftas into the pan. Stir-fry some more, add 425 ml/¾ pint of water, then cover and cook for 20–25 minutes over a low heat.

8 Now add the green chilli and coriander leaves. The consistency of the sauce can be adjusted at this point cooking for a little longer to thicken it or by adding a little boiling water if you prefer a thinner sauce.

Kofta Curry.

VARIATION

KOFTA SAAG
Meatballs with Broccoli or Spinach

SERVES 4

Broccoli is my favourite vegetable and is really good for you too. If you do not share my passion, you can easily substitute fresh spinach.

For this variation, use 285g/10 oz of mince instead and 450 g/1 lb of fresh broccoli (prepared weight), the rest of the ingredients remaining the same as above except that coriander is optional. Follow the method up to step 7 but reserve the green chilli and coriander leaves then continue as follows.

Reduce the heat and drop the grilled Koftas into the pan. Add just 2–3 tablespoons of water and let the Koftas soak up the spices by gently cooking them for 3–4 minutes. Add the broccoli and the green chilli, cover and simmer for 15–20 minutes, stirring occasionally during this time until the moisture disappears. Stir in the coriander leaves just before serving. Adjust the consistency to your taste as above.

FOOD VALUE		
	TOTAL	PER PORTION (¼)
TOTAL FAT	39.8 g	10 g
SATURATED FAT	9 g	2.2 g
CHOLESTEROL	162 mg	40.5 mg
ENERGY (kcals/kj)	872/3648	218/912

GOBHI GOSHT
Lamb with Cauliflower
SERVES 4

INGREDIENTS

450 g/1 lb cauliflower

350 g/¾ lb leg of lamb

2 tbsp oil

75 g/3 oz onion, chopped

½ tsp cumin seeds

2 tsp Ginger and Garlic Paste
(see page 17)

½ tsp chilli powder

¼ tsp turmeric

1 tsp salt

75 g/3 oz tomatoes, chopped

1 tsp grated ginger

½ tsp Garam Masala (see page 18)

3 tbsp coriander leaves, chopped

1 green chilli, chopped

FOOD VALUE

	TOTAL	PER PORTION (¼)
TOTAL FAT	57.3 g	14.3 g
SATURATED FAT	18.3 g	4.6 g
CHOLESTEROL	277 mg	69 mg
ENERGY (kcals/kj)	958/3997	239/999

A very popular everyday dish. Use only the freshest and crispiest cauliflower for the best results.

METHOD

1 Wash the cauliflower and drain it well. Discard the outer leaves and cut the cauliflower into small florets, including all the tender and crispy part of the vegetable, even the young leaves. Cut them into bite-sized pieces.

2 Wash and cut the lamb into 2.5-cm/1-inch cubes.

3 Heat the oil in a medium-sized heavy saucepan. Add the onion and fry it until it is translucent.

4 Add the ground coriander and cumin seeds. Stir-fry them for 30 seconds, then add the Ginger and Garlic Paste, chilli powder, turmeric and salt. Add 2 tablespoons of water and stir continuously. Repeat so that the masala paste turns a shade darker.

5 Then, add the lamb and stir-fry this for 2–3 more minutes. Pour in 240 ml/8 fl oz of water and let it come to the boil, then reduce the heat, cover and simmer for 20–25 minutes.

6 Increase the heat and stir continuously until all the excess moisture has evaporated and the mixture has a slightly glossy look.

7 Add the cauliflower, tomatoes and ginger. Stir to blend everything together, cover and cook briefly (7–8 minutes).

8 Remove the lid, add Garam Masala, half the coriander leaves and the green chilli. Cook, uncovered, to let the liquid escape, turning the vegetables gently, for another 5–7 minutes or until the mixture is really quite dry. Use the remaining coriander leaves to garnish.

Chicken Dishes

MURGH KORMA
Mild, Creamy Chicken Curry
SERVES 4

INGREDIENTS

450 g/1 lb chicken breast
1 tsp chilli powder
1 tsp ground coriander
½ tsp Garam Masala (see page 18)
1 tsp salt
1 tbsp Ginger and Garlic Paste (see page 17)
2 tbsp oil
100 g/¼ lb onion, chopped
3–4 green cardamom pods, slit or bruised
½ tsp cumin seeds
2 tbsp low-fat natural yogurt
fresh mint ot chopped chives, to garnish

FOOD VALUE

	TOTAL	PER PORTION (¼)
TOTAL FAT	37.4 g	9.4 g
SATURATED FAT	7.6 g	1.9 g
CHOLESTEROL	198 mg	50 mg
ENERGY (kcals/kj)	812/3399	203/850

Kormas are mostly rich and exotic. This recipe is for an ordinary, everyday korma, which is delicious even without all the usual trimmings of almonds, cream and lashings of fried onions that normally go with it.

METHOD

1 Wash, bone and cut the chicken into 2.5-cm/1-inch cubes.

2 Put the chilli powder, ground coriander, Garam Masala and salt, plus the Ginger and Garlic Paste into a little bowl. Add 4 tablespoons of hot water, mix and then put the mixture to one side.

3 Heat the oil in a medium-sized heavy saucepan, add the onion, cardamom pods and cumin seeds and fry them gently until the onion turns a deep golden brown.

4 Add the reserved spice mixture, stir it in well and keep cooking over a low heat, sprinkling tiny amounts of water in, if need be, until the paste darkens slightly (this will take 2–3 minutes).

5 Add the chicken, coating it well in the spicy paste. Stir in the yogurt. Cover the pan and simmer for 10 minutes. The chicken will release its own moisture during this time so see how thick or runny the sauce is at the end of it and adjust it by adding water until it is how you like it. Then let it simmer over a low heat for 25–30 minutes. Garnish the finished dish with the mint or chives.

No matter what's been in them, all pots and pans are kept gleaming and clean.

KARAHI CHICKEN
Stir-fried Chicken with Tomatoes
SERVES 4

INGREDIENTS

450 g/1 lb chicken breast

225 g/½ lb tomatoes, chopped

½ tsp chilli powder

2 spring onions, chopped

2 green chillies, chopped

1 tsp salt

2 tbsp oil

1 tsp cumin seeds

2 tsp grated ginger

3–4 cloves garlic, crushed

3 tbsp coriander leaves, chopped

FOOD VALUE

	TOTAL	PER PORTION (¼)
TOTAL FAT	37.3 g	9.3 g
SATURATED FAT	7.3 g	1.8 g
CHOLESTEROL	194 mg	48 mg
ENERGY (kcals/kj)	767/3216	192/804

A quick and easy dish to make, it originates from the north-west frontier of Pakistan. It is usually cooked in a wok-like utensil called a karahi, hence the name of the recipe.

METHOD

1 Wash, bone and cut the chicken into 2.5-cm/1-inch pieces.

2 Put the chicken into a medium-sized heavy saucepan. Cover the pan and leave it to cook in its own moisture over a low heat for about 10 minutes, stirring occasionally.

3 Add the tomatoes, chilli powder, spring onions, green chillies and salt. Cook it, uncovered, over a medium heat for another 15–20 minutes or until the moisture has almost evaporated.

4 Heat the oil in a small frying pan and cook the cumin seeds. As they begin to turn pink, add the ginger and garlic and fry these for about a minute. Add this sizzling mixture to the chicken, together with nearly all the coriander leaves and mix them together well. Simmer for 5–7 minutes. Garnish the dish with the remaining coriander leaves just before serving.

CHICKEN TIKKA
Marinated Grilled Chicken
SERVES 2

INGREDIENTS

2 × 170 g/6 oz chicken breasts

50 g/2 oz onion, chopped

*2 tsp Ginger and Garlic Paste
(see page 17)*

1 green chilli

1 tbsp low-fat natural yogurt

¼–½ tsp chilli powder

¼ tsp Garam Masala (see page 18)

pinch of ground mace

2 tsp lemon juice

2 tbsp coriander leaves, chopped

½ tsp salt

FOOD VALUE

	TOTAL	PER PORTION (½)
TOTAL FAT	8.5 g	4.2 g
SATURATED FAT	2.8 g	1.4 g
CHOLESTEROL	110 mg	55 mg
ENERGY (kcals/kj)	336/1415	168/707

Probably the most popular and best-known dish in the Indian repertoire. As noted before, the skin is removed in most Indian dishes, but in this case no oil is used either, which makes it ideal for our purpose here. It is quite low in calories, too, so I thoroughly recommend that you enjoy it as often as possible.

METHOD

1 Wash, pat dry and skin the chicken breasts. Score them diagonally across in 3–4 places.
2 Combine the remaining ingredients in an electric blender until you have a smooth paste.
3 Spread the spice paste over the chicken pieces, rubbing it well into them. Refrigerate the chicken, preferably overnight, but, if not, for at least 2–3 hours before cooking.
4 Just before you are ready to serve, cook them under a hot grill for 4–5 minutes, then reduce the heat and continue cooking for another 15–20 minutes, turning them over halfway through.

CHICKEN CHANNA
Chicken with Chickpeas
SERVES 4

INGREDIENTS

450 g/1 lb chicken breasts

75 g/3 oz onion, chopped

100 g/¼ lb tomato

1 tbsp Ginger and Garlic Paste
(see page 17)

1 tsp salt

½–1 tsp chilli powder

¼ tsp turmeric

½ tsp Garam Masala (see page 18)

1 tbsp oil

225 g/½ lb chickpeas, tinned, drained

1–2 green chillies

½ tsp cumin seeds, crushed

1 tsp juliennes of fresh ginger

3 tbsp coriander leaves, chopped

2 tsp lemon juice

FOOD VALUE

	TOTAL	PER PORTION (¼)
TOTAL FAT	32.4 g	8.1 g
SATURATED FAT	6.6 g	1.7 g
CHOLESTEROL	194 mg	48 mg
ENERGY (kcals/kj)	924/3888	231/972

This Punjabi invention was incredibly fashionable a few years ago, but, unlike a lot of fashions, this dish has remained popular, no doubt because of its wonderful taste and texture.

METHOD

1 Wash and skin the chicken, then cut it into 2.5-cm/1-inch cubes

2 Put the chicken into a heavy sauce-pan, with the onion, half the tomato and the Ginger and Garlic Paste and salt. Cook over a low heat for 10 minutes or until the chicken releases its moisture, stirring occasionally.

3 Add the chilli powder, turmeric and Garam Masala and cook for a further 10–15 minutes.

4 Add the oil and cook the mixture uncovered until the moisture has almost all evaporated and has a slightly glazed look to it.

5 Add the chickpeas and green chillies. Mix them in well, then add 225–250 ml/7–9 fl oz water. Bring it to the boil and simmer for 7–8 minutes.

6 Lastly, add the cumin seeds, juliennes of ginger, coriander leaves and the lemon juice. Simmer it for a couple more minutes, then garnish the dish with slices of tomatoes, coriander leaves or chopped spring onions.

MURGH SAAG
Chicken with Spinach or Broccoli
SERVES 4

INGREDIENTS

450 g/1 lb chicken breast	
450 g/1 lb fresh spinach or broccoli	
1 tbsp Ginger and Garlic Paste (see page 17)	
50 g/2 oz fenugreek leaves (optional)	
50 g/2 oz onion, chopped	
1 tsp chilli powder	
¼ tsp turmeric	
½ tsp Garam Masala (see page 18)	
½ tsp cumin seeds, crushed	
1 tsp salt	
2 tbsp oil	
1½ tbsp low-fat natural yogurt	
1 green chilli	

FOOD VALUE

	TOTAL	PER PORTION (¼)
TOTAL FAT	40.7 g	10.2 g
SATURATED FAT	8.3 g	2.1 g
CHOLESTEROL	197 mg	49 mg
ENERGY (kcals/kj)	893/3728	223/932

A mainstay of home cooking, this dish pleases everyone in the family. A handful of fresh fenugreek leaves lends a unique, appetizing fragrance to the dish, so do use them if you are able to.

METHOD

1 Wash and skin the chicken and cut it into 2.5 cm/1-inch cubes.

2 Wash the spinach in plenty of running water, carefully removing all the grit, then drain it well.

3 Roughly chop the leaves, discarding the stalks.

4 Pour 115 ml/4 fl oz of water into a medium-sized heavy saucepan. Add the Ginger and Garlic Paste, the onion, chilli powder, turmeric, Garam Masala, cumin seeds and salt. Bring it to the boil, cover and simmer for 3–4 minutes.

5 Drop the chicken pieces into the pan and simmer, uncovered, for 15–20 minutes, or until most of the moisture has evaporated.

6 Add the oil and cook over a higher heat, stirring continuously, until the food looks slightly glazed.

7 Add the yogurt, spinach or broccoli, with the fenugreek, and green chilli. Blend everything well so that the spices coat the spinach evenly. Cover and cook over a low heat for about 10 minutes, or until the spinach releases its own moisture. Remove the lid and simmer uncovered. It is important to note that the Murgh Saag is not ready if it still looks a little watery. The finished dish must be almost dry with a hint of sheen to it.

Fish & Prawn Dishes

Fish Curry

SERVES 4

INGREDIENTS

2 tbsp oil
¼ tsp fenugreek seeds
½ tsp cumin seeds
50 g/2 oz onions, finely chopped
½ tsp chilli powder
¼ tsp turmeric
½ tsp Garam Masala (see page 18)
½ tsp ground coriander
½ tsp salt
2 tbsp low-fat natural yogurt
1 tbsp Ginger and Garlic Paste (see page 17)
450 g/1 lb haddock or cod, cut into 25 g/1 oz chunks
2 tbsp coriander leaves
1–2 green chillies
Mint or chives, chopped, to garnish

FOOD VALUE

	TOTAL	PER PORTION (¼)
TOTAL FAT	26.1 g	6.5 g
SATURATED FAT	3.6 g	0.9 g
CHOLESTEROL	211 mg	53 mg
ENERGY (kcals/kj)	614/2572	154/643

Fenugreek seeds give this curry a special flavour, but take care to use only the amount given as they can make it bitter if used in any quantity.

METHOD

1 Heat the oil in a medium-sized heavy saucepan. Drop in the fenugreek and cumin seeds and fry them for 30 seconds over a medium heat.

2 Add the onion and cook until it turns golden, stirring it from time to time to make sure it does not burn.

3 Blend the chilli powder, turmeric, Garam Masala, ground coriander and salt with the yogurt and then add this spice mixture to the onion. Stir and cook for a minute or so.

4 Add the Ginger and Garlic Paste and cook for a minute or so more. It is important to fry these spices well so that they begin to release their aroma as they darken slightly. Keep stirring, adding a tablespoon or 2 of water occasionally to keep the mixture from burning or sticking. Repeat 2 or 3 times.

5 Drop in the fish pieces, mixing them gently into the cooked masala. Add half the coriander leaves and the green chilli. Reduce the heat, shake the pan, cover, then let it simmer in its own moisture for 20–25 minutes, gently stirring or shaking the pan a couple of times during cooking.

6 Remove the pan from the heat and garnish with the remaining coriander leaves and mint or chives.

KHUTI-MITHI MUCHHLI
Sweet and Sour Fish
SERVES 2

INGREDIENTS

2 × 175 g/6 oz fish fillets
(cod or haddock)

1–2 tbsp Tamarind Pulp (see page 16)

1 tbsp oil

¼ tsp mustard seeds

4–5 curry leaves (optional)

2 spring onions, chopped

½ tsp grated ginger

3 cloves garlic, crushed or chopped

¼ tsp Garam Masala (see page 18)

a pinch turmeric

½ tsp chilli powder

small pinch ground coriander

½ tsp salt

1 tsp sugar

1 green chilli, finely chopped

FOOD VALUE

	TOTAL	PER PORTION (½)
TOTAL FAT	13.7 g	6.8 g
SATURATED FAT	1.7 g	0.8 g
CHOLESTEROL	161 mg	80 mg
ENERGY (kcals/kj)	394/1656	197/414

The sweet and sour taste is created by the liberal use of tamarind. If you cannot find tamarind, try vinegar or lemon juice instead.

METHOD

1 Cut the fish into 5-cm/2-inch chunks and smother them with the tamarind pulp, to which has been added a pinch of salt. Set the fish to one side to marinate.

2 Heat the oil in a medium-sized heavy saucepan. Add the mustard seeds and curry leaves, if using, and stir-fry them until they begin to crackle.

3 Add the spring onion (reserving the pieces of green shoot). Soften the spring onion and add the ginger, garlic, Garam Masala, turmeric, chilli powder, ground coriander and salt. Cook this mixture well, adding a tablespoon of water from time to time until the masala paste turns slightly darker (1–2 minutes).

4 Add the fish pieces, sugar and green chilli, stirring gently. Cover the pan and let the fish cook over a medium heat for 8–10 minutes, occasionally shaking the pan to make sure it does not stick (add a little more water if you prefer a runny sauce).

MUCHHLI AUR SUBZI
Fish with Vegetables
SERVES 4

INGREDIENTS

450 g/1 lb fish, frozen or fresh; haddock or cod
100 g/¼ lb runner beans
2 tbsp oil
½ tsp mustard seeds
½ tsp cumin seeds
¼ tsp fenugreek seeds
1 tsp grated ginger
100 g/¼ lb cauliflower florets
75 g/3 oz tomatoes
½ tsp chilli powder
¼ tsp turmeric
¼ tsp Garam Masala (see page 18)
½ tsp salt
3–4 cloves garlic, crushed
2 tsp lemon juice
1 green chilli, chopped
2 tbsp coriander leaves

FOOD VALUE

	TOTAL	PER PORTION (¼)
TOTAL FAT	26.8 g	6.7 g
SATURATED FAT	3.5 g	0.9 g
CHOLESTEROL	207 mg	52 mg
ENERGY (kcals/kj)	611/2557	153/639

This is cooked Bengali style. Traditionally mustard oil is used but, if you cannot find it, you can substitute any vegetable oil in its place. If you do use mustard oil, you must heat it to smoking point otherwise its pungent smell and taste will overpower the fish and can ruin the dish.

METHOD

1 Wash and pat the fish dry. Cut it into 2.5-cm/1-inch pieces.

2 Top and tail the beans and cut them into 1-cm/½-inch lengths.

3 Heat the oil in a medium-sized heavy saucepan and add the mustard, cumin and fenugreek seeds. Stir-fry them until they begin to pop and splutter.

4 Add the ginger and fry it for a minute or so. Then add the beans, cauliflower and tomatoes, mix them in and cook for a couple of minutes.

5 Add the chilli powder, turmeric, Garam Masala and salt, mix them well in, then cover the pan and cook over a low heat for 10–12 minutes.

6 Make a well in the centre of the vegetables and gently drop in the fish pieces, add the garlic, lemon juice, green chilli and half the coriander leaves, then cover them with the vegetables. Simmer, covered, for 15–20 minutes, stirring gently halfway through.

7 Add the remaining coriander leaves, shake the pan and let it stand for a couple of minutes before serving.

Goan Fish Curry
SERVES 4

INGREDIENTS

6–7 whole dried chillies
½ tsp coriander seeds
½ tsp cumin seeds
6–7 cloves garlic, crushed
½ tsp salt
1 tbsp desiccated coconut
450 g/1 lb haddock or cod fillets
50 g/2 oz onion, chopped
2 tbsp oil
1 tsp grated ginger
75 g/3 oz tomatoes, chopped
1–2 green chillies
1 tbsp Tamarind Pulp (see page 16) or vinegar

FOOD VALUE

	TOTAL	PER PORTION (¼)
TOTAL FAT	34.8 g	8.7 g
SATURATED FAT	11.3 g	2.8 g
CHOLESTEROL	207 mg	52 mg
ENERGY (kcals/kj)	661/2766	165/692

Like most Goan curries, this dish is a bit hot. You could, of course, tame it according to your own taste simply by reducing the number of whole dried chillies you use.

METHOD

1 Grind the whole dried chillies, coriander and cumin seeds, garlic and salt together to form a paste.

2 Soak the coconut in 4 tablespoons of warm water for 15 minutes.

3 Cut the fish into 2.5-cm/1-inch pieces.

4 Sauté the onion in the oil over a medium heat until it turns golden brown. Add the spice paste and fry it well, adding a tiny amount of water frequently until it turns a slightly darker colour (this should take about 1–2 minutes).

5 Add the grated ginger, chopped tomatoes and green chillies. Mix them gently in, then drop in the fish pieces. Stir lightly to coat the fish pieces with the spices, then simmer for 5 minutes.

6 Add the soaked coconut and Tamarind Pulp or vinegar and let it simmer for 10–12 minutes, adding a little more liquid if you like a runny sauce or letting it cook uncovered for a couple more minutes if you prefer it thicker.

Fish Kebabs

SERVES 4

INGREDIENTS

400 g/14 oz fresh or frozen haddock or cod

2–3 tbsp coriander leaves or mint
or chives, chopped

1 tbsp lemon juice

1-cm/½-inch piece cinnamon stick

2–3 cloves

1 black cardamom pod, bruised (optional)

1 tsp grated ginger

4 cloves garlic, crushed

175 g/6 oz mashed potato

½ tsp chilli powder

½ tsp salt

1 green chilli, chopped

2 tsp oil

1 size 3 egg, beaten

chopped spring onion and wedges of fresh
lemon, to garnish

FOOD VALUE

	TOTAL	PER PORTION (¼)
TOTAL FAT	15.2 g	1.9 g
SATURATED FAT	2.9 g	0.4 g
CHOLESTEROL	403 mg	50 mg
ENERGY (kcals/kj)	568/2395	71/299

METHOD

1 Rinse the fish under running cold water.

2 Put the mint or chives into a small bowl, mix in the lemon juice and season, then put the mixture to one side.

3 In a small saucepan, put the cinnamon, cloves and cardamom pod and 100 ml/4 fl oz of slightly salted water, together with the ginger and garlic. Let it come to the boil gradually.

4 Put the fish into the spiced water and cook, uncovered, over a medium heat. Cook until the fish is tender and the water has completely evaporated. Leave it to cool, then discard the spices.

5 Flake the fish, removing any bones. Add the mashed potato, chilli powder, salt, green chilli and coriander leaves and mix them together.

6 Divide the mixture into 8 portions and roll each one into a neat ball with moistened hands. Make a dent in each ball, put a small quantity of the lemon mixture into it, cover the mixture then flatten into a burger shape. Keep them in the fridge until you are ready to serve them.

7 Grease a fairly large, preferably non-stick, frying pan with half the oil. Dip each Kebab into the beaten egg and put them into the hot pan. Fry them in 2 batches of 4, turning them only once. They should be completely heated through and look golden and crispy. Serve them piping hot, garnishing with the chopped coriander or chives and a wedge of fresh lemon.

The beaches of Goa are amongst the most beautiful in the world. Its waters are plentiful in fish and you will find the most delicious seafood dishes in this region.

MASALA MUCHHLI
Masala Fish
SERVES 2

INGREDIENTS

285 g/10 oz haddock or cod fish steaks

1 tbsp oil

2 spring onions

1 tsp Ginger and Garlic Paste
(see page 17)

1 tbsp low-fat natural yogurt

MARINADE

¼ tsp garlic powder

2 tsp lemon juice

freshly ground black pepper
and salt to taste

MASALA PASTE

8 fenugreek seeds

¼ tsp cumin seeds

1 tsp Ginger and Garlic Paste
(see page 17)

¼ tsp chilli powder

a pinch turmeric

a pinch Garam Masala (see page 18)

1 tbsp low-fat natural yogurt

a pinch salt

1 tbsp coriander leaves

lemon wedges, to garnish

FOOD VALUE

	TOTAL	PER PORTION (½)
TOTAL FAT	13.2 g	6.6 g
SATURATED FAT	1.8 g	0.9 g
CHOLESTEROL	106 mg	53 mg
ENERGY (kcals/kj)	307/1288	153/644

METHOD

1 Put the fish in a shallow dish. Mix the marinade ingredients together and pour the mixture over the fish. Ensure it is well covered, then leave it to marinate in the fridge for at least 2–3 hours before cooking.

2 Heat the oil in a small saucepan. Add the cumin and fenugreek seeds and fry them for a minute. Then add all the other masala paste ingredients, except the coriander and lemon wedges, and stir continuously. Add 1 tablespoon of water from time to time to stop it sticking and cook for at least 2–3 minutes. Lastly, add the coriander leaves and remove the pan from the heat.

3 Just before serving, place the fish under a hot grill for 8–10 minutes, turning once. Heat the masala paste and add 3–4 tbsp of water. Let it come to the boil, stir in the spring onions and switch off. Transfer the fish onto a serving plate, pour over the hot masala and garnish with onion shoots or coriander leaves and lemon wedges.

Grilled Masala Fish

SERVES 1

INGREDIENTS

145 g/5 oz any white-fleshed fish (coley, haddock or cod)
1 tsp lemon juice
a pinch garlic powder
salt to taste
2 tsp low-fat natural yogurt
½ tsp Ginger and Garlic Paste (see page 17)
a pinch chilli powder
a pinch Garam Masala (see page 18)
1 tbsp mint or coriander leaves, chopped
½ tsp oil
lemon wedges to garnish

FOOD VALUE

	TOTAL	SINGLE PORTION
TOTAL FAT		2.9 g
SATURATED FAT		0.5 g
CHOLESTEROL		70 mg
ENERGY (kcals/kj)		146/617

After being marinated, this fish is usually deep- or shallow-fried, but it is still delicious when just lightly brushed with oil and cooked under a hot grill.

METHOD

1 Wash and pat the fish dry.

2 Mix the lemon juice, garlic powder and a pinch of salt together and rub this mixture over the fish. Leave in the fridge for 15–20 minutes.

3 Combine the yogurt, Ginger and Garlic Paste, chilli powder, Garam Masala, mint or coriander leaves, reserving a little for garnishing, and a little salt. Add the oil to this masala paste and blend thoroughly.

4 Coat the fish, on both sides, with the masala paste and leave it to marinate a second time in the fridge for at least an hour.

5 Put the fish under a hot grill and cook for 4–5 minutes on each side. Garnish with the lemon wedges and reserved mint or coriander leaves.

Spicy Sardine Spread

SERVES 2

INGREDIENTS

100 g/¼ lb sardines in tomato sauce

2 green chillies, thinly sliced

2–3 cloves garlic, finely chopped

2 spring onions

1 tbsp mint or coriander leaves

a pinch freshly ground black pepper

1 tsp vinegar or lemon juice

a pinch salt

50 g/2 oz onion, chopped

75 g/3 oz cucumber, sliced

FOOD VALUE

	TOTAL	PORTION (½)
TOTAL FAT	12 g	6 g
SATURATED FAT	3.3 g	1.6 g
CHOLESTEROL	76 mg	38 mg
ENERGY (kcals/kj)	211/884	105/442

No cooking is required for this instantaneous, simple and "just out of the larder" spread. I invent things like this on an impulse, wanting to get the best out of simple ingredients with the minimum fuss.

METHOD

1 Flake the sardines into a bowl and add the green chillies, garlic, spring onion, mint or coriander leaves and freshly ground pepper to it.

2 Pour the vinegar or lemon juice over the sardine mixture. Sprinkle the salt onto the onion and cucumber and add these to the sardine mixture, too. Mix thoroughly. This is delicious on toasted bread, or as a sandwich filling.

JHINGA ALOO

Prawns with Potatoes

SERVES 4

INGREDIENTS

350 g/¾ lb prawns, fresh or frozen

1 tbsp lemon juice

¼ tsp garlic powder or fresh crushed garlic

225 g/½ lb potatoes

2 tbsp oil

¼ tsp fenugreek seeds

½ tsp cumin seeds

75 g/3 oz tomatoes, chopped

½ tsp chilli powder

¼ tsp turmeric

¼ tsp Garam Masala (see page 18)

1–2 green chillies, chopped

2 tsp Ginger & Garlic Paste (see page 17)

½ tsp salt

3 tbsp coriander leaves, chopped

FOOD VALUE

	TOTAL	PER PORTION
TOTAL FAT	29.2 g	7.3 g
SATURATED FAT	4.2 g	1.05 g
CHOLESTEROL	284 mg	71 mg
ENERGY (kcals/kj)	762/3198	191/800

METHOD

1 Wash and pat the prawns dry.

2 Mix the lemon juice and garlic powder or fresh garlic together and coat the prawns with the mixture. Leave them to marinate, refrigerated, for 20 minutes.

3 Chop the potatoes into 1-cm/½-inch dice, preferably with skins.

4 Heat the oil in a medium-sized heavy saucepan, then add the fenugreek and cumin seeds, letting them sizzle for half a minute.

5 Add the Ginger and Garlic Paste and cook for 30 seconds, then add the potato and tomato. Stir and cook them for 2 minutes.

6 Now add the marinated prawns. Mix them in and, immediately, add the chilli powder, turmeric, Garam Masala, green chillies and salt. Mix thoroughly, then add 140 ml/¼ pt of hot water. Cover the pan and simmer for 8–10 minutes, or until the potato is just tender – do not let them become overdone.

7 Add half the coriander leaves, stirring them into the curry and cook for a minute or 2.

8 Sprinkle the remaining coriander leaves over the top to garnish and remove the pan from the heat.

BHOONA JHINGA
Dry Masala Prawns
SERVES 4

INGREDIENTS

½ tsp cumin seeds

½ tsp coriander seeds

1 tsp aniseed

3–4 whole dried chillies

4–5 cloves garlic, chopped

1–2 green chillies, chopped

50 g/2 oz onion, chopped

2 tbsp coriander leaves

2 tbsp oil

¼ tsp fenugreek seeds

450 g/1 lb prawns

75 g/3 oz tomatoes

1 tbsp low-fat yogurt

¼ tsp turmeric

coriander or mint leaves, to garnish

FOOD VALUE

	TOTAL	PER PORTION (¼)
TOTAL FAT	30.8 g	7.7 g
SATURATED FAT	4.8 g	1.2 g
CHOLESTEROL	367 mg	92 mg
ENERGY (kcals/kj)	739/3090	185/773

An absolutely delicious south-Indian prawn dish.

METHOD

1 Dry roast the cumin and coriander seeds and aniseed in a small, heavy frying pan over a low heat for a couple of minutes, then leave them to cool. Grind them together with the whole dried chillies, garlic, green chillies, onion and coriander leaves.

2 Heat the oil in a heavy saucepan and fry the fenugreek seeds for half a minute. Add the prawns, tomato and yogurt. Cook over a high heat for 1 minute to seal them.

3 Now add the ground spice mixture and the turmeric. Mix them in well and fry for another minute.

4 Add 100 ml/4 fl oz of water and bring to the boil. Lower the heat and simmer for 5–7 minutes. Garnish with 1 tbsp mint or coriander leaves.

Goan Prawn Curry

SERVES 4

INGREDIENTS

3–4 whole dried chillies
¼ tsp peppercorns
½ tsp cumin seeds
1 tsp coriander seeds
1 tbsp fresh or desiccated coconut
4–5 cloves garlic, chopped
2 tbsp oil
75 g/3 oz onions
75 g/3 oz tomatoes
2 tsp grated ginger
1–2 green chillies
2 tbsp Tamarind Pulp (see page 16) or 1 tbsp vinegar
450 g/1 lb prawns
2 tbsp coriander leaves, chopped

FOOD VALUE

	TOTAL	PER PORTION (¼)
TOTAL FAT	39.8 g	10 g
SATURATED FAT	12.6 g	3.2 g
CHOLESTEROL	365 mg	91 mg
ENERGY (kcals/kj)	810/3385	202/846

I was first introduced to this dish by my Goan friend at an office party, and it soon became one of our family favourites. It may well become one of your favourites too! This is, of course, slightly modified to reduce the calories but I still find it tasty enough to want you to try it. The original recipe calls for huge amounts of fresh, grated coconut, but I find that just the single spoonful we are allowed here is satisfying enough.

METHOD

1 Grind together the whole dried chillies, peppercorns and cumin and coriander seeds. Then add the coconut and garlic and grind some more.

2 Heat the oil in a medium-sized saucepan and fry the onions over low heat. As they begin to turn translucent, add the ginger and green chillies and cook for half a minute. Add the spice paste, with the salt, mix this masala in and fry it for about a minute, adding a little water.

3 Add the Tamarind Pulp or vinegar stirring continuously for half a minute.

4 Stir in the prawns and tomatoes and coat them well in the sauce. Add 100–150 ml/4–6 fl oz of water and let the curry cook for 5 minutes over a medium heat.

5 Add most of the coriander leaves and simmer for another 5–7 minutes. Garnish with the remaining coriander leaves.

JHINGA SUBZI
Prawn Curry with Vegetables
SERVES 4

INGREDIENTS

285 g/10 oz prawns, fresh or frozen
75 g/3 oz green beans, fresh or frozen
2 tbsp oil
50 g/2 oz onion, finely chopped
1 tsp grated ginger
½ tsp chilli powder
¼ tsp turmeric
¼ tsp Garam Masala (see page 18)
1 tsp salt
50 g/2 oz tomato, chopped
75 g/3 oz red peppers, chopped
75 g/3 oz button mushrooms
3–4 cloves garlic, chopped
1–2 green chillies, chopped
½ tsp sugar
1 tbsp low-fat natural yogurt
2 tbsp coriander leaves, chopped

FOOD VALUE

	TOTAL	PER PORTION (¼)
TOTAL FAT	28.6 g	7.2 g
SATURATED FAT	4.2 g	1 g
CHOLESTEROL	225 mg	56 mg
ENERGY (kcals/kj)	595/2487	149/622

You can choose your own combination of vegetables for this dish – just check the calories for the selected vegetables.

METHOD

1 If using fresh prawns, wash and pat them dry.

2 If using fresh green beans, wash then cut them into small bite-size lengths.

3 Heat the oil in a medium-sized heavy saucepan and fry the onion and, as it turns translucent, add the ginger, chilli powder, turmeric, Garam Masala and salt. Mix well and cook for a few seconds.

4 Now add the tomato, red pepper and mushrooms, stir and cook for 5–7 minutes over a medium heat.

5 Add the prawns, garlic, green chillies, sugar and yogurt. Mix well and cook over a medium heat for 7–8 minutes.

6 Add the coriander leaves and simmer for another couple of minutes.

BHINDI JHINGA
Prawns with Okra
SERVES 4

INGREDIENTS

350 g/¾ lb okra (prepared weight)
2 tbsp oil
100 g/¼ lb onions
2–3 whole dried chillies
½ tsp cumin seeds
4 cloves garlic, chopped
¼ tsp turmeric
½ tsp chilli powder
100 g/¼ lb tomatoes, chopped
225 g/½ lb prawns
1–2 green chillies, slit
1 tsp salt
2 tbsp Tamarind Pulp (see page 16)
2 tbsp coriander leaves, chopped

FOOD VALUE

	TOTAL	PER PORTION (¼)
TOTAL FAT	27.8 g	7 g
SATURATED FAT	4 g	1 g
CHOLESTEROL	450 mg	113 mg
ENERGY (kcals/kj)	523/2187	131/546

METHOD

1 Wash and pat the okra dry. Top and tail them and chop them into 1-cm/½-inch wide slices.

2 Heat the oil and lightly fry the onion with the dried chillies and cumin seeds and then add the garlic, turmeric, chilli powder and ginger.

Stir them together well and cook the mixture for a couple of minutes, stirring continuously.

3 Add the okra and tomato, coat them well with the spices, cover the pan and simmer gently for 5–7 minutes, stirring occasionally.

4 Stir in the prawns, chopped or slit green chillies and salt. Cook for another 5 minutes, then add the Tamarind Pulp or lemon juice and coriander leaves. Shake the pan and simmer for 5 more minutes. Then, turn off the heat and let it stand for 2–3 minutes before serving.

Prawns with Okra.

JHINGA SAAG
Prawns with Broccoli or Spinach
SERVES 4

450 g/1 lb broccoli or fresh spinach	
2 tsp Ginger and Garlic Paste (see page 17)	
2 tbsp oil	
50 g/2 oz onion, finely chopped	
¼ tsp cumin seeds	
2 cloves garlic, finely chopped	
½ tsp chilli powder	
¼ tsp turmeric	
½ tsp Garam Masala (see page 18)	
¾ tsp salt	
285 g/10 oz prawns, fresh or frozen	
1 tbsp low-fat natural yogurt	
50 g/2 oz tomato, chopped	

FOOD VALUE

	TOTAL	PER PORTION (¼)
TOTAL FAT	31.7 g	7.9 g
SATURATED FAT	4.9 g	1.2 g
CHOLESTEROL	225 mg	56 mg
ENERGY (kcals/kj)	695/2902	174/726

METHOD

1 If using fresh prawns, wash and pat them dry.

2 Wash and chop the broccoli or spinach.

3 Put the broccoli or spinach into a medium-sized saucepan and add the Ginger and Garlic Paste, a pinch of salt and 100 ml/4 fl oz of water. Cook, uncovered, over a low heat until the broccoli or spinach is tender and almost all of the liquid has evaporated.

4 Heat the oil in another medium-sized heavy saucepan. Fry the onion and cumin seeds until they change to a pale gold colour.

5 Add the garlic and cook for 30 seconds, then add the chilli powder, turmeric, Garam Masala and salt. Cook this mixture for another minute or so, adding 1 tablespoon of water as necessary to avoid the mixture burning or sticking, and stir continuously.

6 Add the prawns and then the yogurt. Stir-fry everything together for half a minute.

7 Add the tomato, mix it in and cook over a low heat for 2–3 minutes. Combine the cooked broccoli with the prawn mixture and cook over a medium heat for another 8–10 minutes.

SAAG

PUNCHMAIL BHAJI

PHALLI ALOO

SEASONAL VEGETABLES IN GREEN MASALA

Vegetable Dishes

CABBAGE AND CARROT BHAJI

BANGON ALOO

MUSHROOM, LEEK AND PEPPER BHAJI

QUICK CRUNCHY BHAJI

ALOO KA BHURTA

MUTTER MUSHROOM BHAJI

DUM GOBHI

PALAK ALOO

SAAG
Greens with Garlic Butter

SERVES 4

INGREDIENTS

400 g/14 oz fresh broccoli
400 g/14 oz fresh spinach
2 tsp grated ginger
2–3 green chillies, chopped
½ tsp salt
3 tbsp sterilised tinned cream
25 g/1 oz butter
5–6 plump cloves garlic, crushed

FOOD VALUE

	TOTAL	PER PORTION (¼)
TOTAL FAT	36.2 g	9.05 g
SATURATED FAT	20.3 g	5.1 g
CHOLESTEROL	82 mg	21 mg
ENERGY (kcals/kj)	506/2091	127/523

This is a typically Punjabi dish, cooked with hardly any spices at all. In the villages of the Punjab, it is served on a firm disc-like roti, made from coarsely ground maize, called Mukki ki roti. The Saag is topped with home-made butter and accompanied by either a tall glass of freshly made frothy lassi or sugarcane juice – absolutely superb and very energizing.

Traditionally, Saag is mainly made with mustard leaves, which can occasionally be seen at Asian grocers, but, if you are not one of their regular customers with a sharp sense of curiosity, you could easily miss them. Turnip tops are a good alternative, but they are just as scarce. I have discovered, though, that a combination of broccoli and spinach makes the best match in terms of flavour and texture. The addition of broccoli, in particular, works really well; not only does it shorten the cooking time, it also helps to bring out that special, melting smoothness that is the best part about the traditional recipe.

METHOD

1 Wash the greens thoroughly and then chop them finely, discarding the spinach stalks, but using every bit of the broccoli.

2 Pour 240 ml/8 fl oz of water into a heavy saucepan, then add the greens, ginger, green chillies and salt and bring it to the boil over a medium heat.

3 Reduce the heat, cover the pan and simmer for 30–35 minutes or until the greens are completely tender.

4 Remove the lid and, using a wooden spoon, mash the vegetables as much as you possibly can and evaporate excess moisture at the same time. Continue cooking the Saag until it has a mushy, almost puréed look.

5 Stir in the cream and let it simmer for a few more minutes.

6 Heat the butter in a small frying pan and add the garlic. As soon as it turns pink/translucent, pour this sizzling mixture over the greens and mix it in thoroughly. Let it stand briefly so that the aroma and flavour of the garlic and butter seeps well into the Saag.

PUNCHMAIL BHAJI

Mixed Vegetable Bhaji

PUNCHMAIL BHAJI

SERVES 4

INGREDIENTS

100 g/¼ lb green beans
175 g/6 oz potatoes
100 g/¼ lb carrots
175 g/6 oz aubergine
100 g/¼ lb tomatoes
1–2 green chillies
2 tbsp oil
7–8 cloves garlic, finely chopped
½ tsp chilli powder
¼ tsp turmeric powder
½–¾ tsp salt
2–3 tbsp mint or coriander leaves

FOOD VALUE

	TOTAL	PER PORTION (¼)
TOTAL FAT	24 g	6 g
SATURATED FAT	3 g	0.8 g
CHOLESTEROL	0	0
ENERGY (kcals/kj)	409/1702	102/426

The word "Punchmail" means "the mixture of five". The best thing about this dish is that every time it is cooked, it has a new taste as the combination of the five vegetables is somehow never quite the same. It is also a very simple and quick way of making a Bhaji and yet so tasty.

METHOD

1 Top and tail and de-string the beans, then chop them into bite-size lengths.

2 Cut the potatoes into quarters and halve them again, preferably leaving the skin on.

3 Scrape and dice the carrots.

4 Cut the aubergine into 4 strips lengthwise and then slice across into 1-cm/½-inch chunks.

5 Roughly chop the tomatoes and green chillies.

6 Measure the oil into a medium-sized heavy saucepan over a medium heat. Add the garlic, stirring it as soon as it begins to turn translucent, then add all the vegetables. Also stir in the chilli powder, turmeric and salt. Mix the spices together thoroughly.

7 Lower the heat, cover the pan and cook for another 20–25 minutes.

8 Add the mint or coriander leaves, stir and switch the heat off. Let it stand for 2–3 minutes before serving.

PHALLI ALOO
Green Beans with Potatoes
SERVES 4

INGREDIENTS

400 g/14 oz runner beans

200 g/7 oz potatoes

2 tbsp oil

½ tsp cumin seeds

3–4 whole dried chillies or
½ tsp chilli powder

75 g/3 oz tomato, chopped

1–2 green chillies

¼ tsp turmeric

salt to taste

FOOD VALUE

	TOTAL	PER PORTION (¼)
TOTAL FAT	24.6 g	6.2 g
SATURATED FAT	3.1 g	0.8 g
CHOLESTEROL	0	0
ENERGY (kcals/kj)	457/1899	114/475

METHOD

1 Top and tail the runner beans and chop them into small pieces.

2 Scrub the potatoes and dice finely, preferably keeping the skin on.

3 Heat the oil, add the cumin seeds and break in the whole dried chillies (if using the chilli powder, do not add it yet).

4 As soon as the dried chillies darken (this just takes a minute or so), add the runner beans, tomato and green chillies. Cook for a couple of minutes, then add the potato. Add the chilli powder now, if using, together with the turmeric and salt. Cover and simmer for 15 minutes.

Seasonal Vegetables in Green Masala
SERVES 4

INGREDIENTS

225 g/½ lb cauliflower

100 g/¼ lb green beans

100 g/¼ lb carrots

100 g/¼ lb red or green peppers

100 g/¼ lb tomatoes

2 green chillies

3 tbsp coriander leaves

2 tbsp oil

3–4 whole dried chillies

1 tsp cumin seeds

¼ tsp turmeric

½–¾ tsp salt

2 tsp grated ginger

4–5 fat cloves garlic, chopped

FOOD VALUE

	TOTAL	PER PORTION (¼)
TOTAL FAT	25.4 g	6.4 g
SATURATED FAT	3.4 g	0.8 g
CHOLESTEROL	0	0
ENERGY (kcals/kj)	364/1513	91/378

I have chosen 4 vegetables, but you can substitute any you prefer or happen to have. If one of them happens to be potatoes, however, remember that they are higher in calories, but this is quite low in calories so, if you are not watching them too closely, this will be all right.

METHOD

1 Remove the outer leaves from the cauliflower and cut it into florets.

2 Top and tail and de-string the green beans, then chop them into bite-size lengths.

3 Scrape, wash and dice the carrots.

4 Cut the peppers into tiny squares.

5 Chop the tomatoes, green chillies and coriander leaves.

6 Heat the oil in a medium-sized heavy saucepan. Break and drop the whole dried chillies into the pan (do not put the chilli powder in yet, if using) together with the cumin seeds and, within a minute of adding these, add all the vegetables (but not the green chillies or coriander leaves). At the same time, add the turmeric, chilli powder, if using, and salt. Cook for a minute or so while stirring the vegetables together.

7 Now add the ginger, garlic, green chillies, and coriander leaves (which together are the green masala). Stir continuously until the ingredients are well mixed. Cover the pan and simmer over a medium heat for 15 minutes, until the vegetables are just slightly underdone.

Seasonal Vegetables in Green Masala.

Cabbage and Carrot Bhaji

SERVES 4

INGREDIENTS

2 tbsp oil
1 tbsp coriander seeds, crushed
½ tsp cumin seeds
2–3 whole dried chillies
350 g/¾ lb cabbage, shredded
175 g/6 oz carrots, diced
75 g/3 oz tomatoes, chopped
¼ tsp turmeric
1 green chilli, chopped
½ tsp salt

FOOD VALUE

	TOTAL	PER PORTION (¼)
TOTAL FAT	24 g	6 g
SATURATED FAT	3 g	0.8 g
CHOLESTEROL	0	0
ENERGY (kcals/kj)	350/1446	88/362

This is a sheer blessing for slimmers! It is very simple and quick to make and tastes really good. It is a money, time and calorie saver – what more can one ask for?

METHOD

1 Heat the oil in a medium-sized heavy saucepan and stir in the coriander and cumin seeds and whole dried chillies (if using chilli powder instead, do not add it at this stage). Fry these over a medium heat for a minute, or until the chillies and seeds darken slightly.

2 Add the cabbage, carrot and tomatoes, then the turmeric, chilli powder, if using, green chillies and salt. Stir to mix everything together thoroughly.

3 Reduce the heat, cover and simmer for 15–20 minutes. The vegetables should be on the very edge of tender with a little crunch to them, but if you like your vegetables softer, cook them for a little longer.

Vegetable vendors compete fiercely to sell their produce.

BANGON ALOO
Aubergine with Potatoes
SERVES 4

INGREDIENTS

INGREDIENTS
350 g/¾ lb aubergine
225 g/½ lb potatoes
2 tbsp oil
50 g/2 oz onion, sliced
½ tsp cumin seeds
½ tsp Roasted and Crushed Coriander Seeds (see page 18)
3–4 curry leaves (optional)
1 tsp grated ginger
4–5 cloves garlic, finely chopped
½ tsp chilli powder
¼ tsp turmeric
salt to taste
1 tbsp low-fat natural yogurt
½ tsp sugar
1–2 green chillies, chopped
75 g/3 oz tomato, chopped
1 tbsp lemon juice
2 tbsp coriander leaves, chopped

FOOD VALUE

	TOTAL	PER PORTION (¼)
TOTAL FAT	24.8 g	6.2 g
SATURATED FAT	3.3 g	0.8 g
CHOLESTEROL	2 mg	0.5 mg
ENERGY (kcals/kj)	496/2174	124/544

METHOD

1 Wash the aubergine. Cut it into quarters lengthwise, then, holding the pieces together, cut them across into 1-cm/½-inch chunks.

2 Scrub the potatoes thoroughly and do not peel them, then cut each one into quarters and each quarter twice or more so that you have at least 12 bite-size pieces, from each potato.

3 Heat the oil in a medium-sized heavy saucepan and fry the onion until it turns a light brown colour.

4 Add the cumin and coriander seeds and the curry leaves, if using. Fry these for a minute or so, then add the ginger, half the garlic, the chilli powder, turmeric and salt. Cook this mixture over quite a high heat, adding 2 tablespoons of water as necessary so that the spice paste deepens in colour and does not stick (this should not take longer than 2 minutes).

5 Add the aubergine, then the yogurt, sugar and green chillies. Mix everything together and cook for 2–3 minutes. Add 140 ml/¼ pint of water, lower the heat and simmer for 15 minutes, with the lid firmly on.

6 Add the potato, peppers and tomato. Ensuring that the lid is firmly on, simmer for another 10 minutes, checking it occasionally to make sure that it is not sticking or burning. If it seems a bit too dry or you would prefer a little more sauce, just add a little more water and let it simmer for a few more minutes.

7 Lastly, add the remaining garlic, the lemon juice and coriander leaves. Cook for 1 more minute, gently stir to mix it thoroughly, then turn off the heat.

Mushroom, Leek and Pepper Bhaji

SERVES 4

INGREDIENTS

350 g/¾ lb mushrooms (prepared weight)

50 g/2 oz leek

2 tsp coriander seeds

½ tsp cumin seeds

3 tbsp oil

2 tsp low-fat natural yogurt

3–4 plump cloves garlic, finely chopped

50 g/2 oz red pepper, sliced

50 g/2 oz green pepper, sliced

½ tsp chilli powder

¼ tsp turmeric

½ tsp salt

50 g/2 oz tomato, chopped

1–2 green chilli, very finely chopped

2 tbsp coriander leaves

FOOD VALUE

	TOTAL	PER PORTION (¼)
TOTAL FAT	35.9 g	9 g
SATURATED FAT	4.6 g	1.2 g
CHOLESTEROL	1.3 mg	0.3 mg
ENERGY (kcals/kj)	403/1670	101/418

METHOD

1 Wipe the mushrooms clean and pull out their stalks. Cut the small mushrooms in half and the large ones into quarters.

2 Wash the leek thoroughly and cut into 5-mm/¼-inch thick slices.

3 Crush the coriander seeds with a rolling pin and set them to one side.

4 Add the coriander and cumin seeds to the oil, which has been heated in a pan, and let them sizzle for 30 seconds over a medium heat.

5 Add the yogurt, garlic and the prepared vegetables. Stir to mix everything together, then cook for 1–2 minutes.

6 Add the chilli powder, turmeric and salt, stirring continuously as you do so.

7 Add the tomato and green chilli and cook, uncovered, over a medium heat for 8–10 minutes, stirring from time to time and evaporating as much moisture as possible.

8 Add half the coriander leaves, stirring them into the mixture, then garnish the dish with the remaining leaves.

The Taj Mahal at dawn.

Quick, Crunchy Bhaji

SERVES 4

INGREDIENTS

100 g/¼ lb cauliflower
100 g/¼ lb green beans
100 g/¼ lb red and green peppers
3 tbsp oil
3–4 whole dried chillies, broken roughly
1 tsp cumin seeds
¼ tsp turmeric
½ tsp salt
100 g/¼ lb carrots
100 g/¼ lb tomatoes, chopped
2 tsp grated ginger
3–4 plump cloves garlic, chopped or crushed
1 green chilli, chopped
2–3 tbsp coriander leaves, chopped

FOOD VALUE

	TOTAL	PER PORTION (¼)
TOTAL FAT	35.3 g	8.8 g
SATURATED FAT	4.5 g	1.1 g
CHOLESTEROL	0	0
ENERGY (kcals/kj)	421/1742	105/436

METHOD

1 Cut the cauliflower into small florets.

2 Trim the green beans and cut each one into 3–4 pieces.

3 Cut the red and green peppers into small squares.

4 Scrub and dice the carrots.

5 Heat the oil in a medium-sized heavy pan, then add the whole dried chillies, breaking them into the pan, and the cumin seeds. As they begin to sizzle, add the turmeric and salt. Stir, then add all the vegetables, including the tomato. Mix and simmer for 2 minutes.

6 Add the ginger, garlic and green chillies and stir to blend everything together thoroughly.

7 Then, lower the heat, cover the pan tightly and steam cook the vegetables for 12–15 minutes.

8 Finally, add the coriander leaves, then serve.

ALOO KA BHURTA
Broken Potatoes with Spices
SERVES 4

INGREDIENTS

350 g/¾ lb potatoes
2 tbsp oil
75 g/3 oz onions, chopped
½ tsp cumin seeds
2–3 whole dried chillies, broken
¼ tsp turmeric
75 g/3 oz tomatoes, chopped
1 green chilli, chopped
½ tsp salt
3 tbsp coriander leaves, chopped

FOOD VALUE

	TOTAL	PER PORTION (¼)
TOTAL FAT	23.2 g	5.8 g
SATURATED FAT	2.7 g	0.7 g
CHOLESTEROL	0	0
ENERGY (kcals/kj)	519/2173	130/543

METHOD

1 Boil the potatoes in their skins and leave them to cool. Then, peel and break them into a lumpy mash. If preferred, peel potatoes first and then boil.

2 Heat the oil in a medium-sized heavy saucepan and add the onion, cumin seeds and whole dried chillies, breaking them into the pan. Fry until the onions turn a rich, golden brown.

3 Add the mashed potato. Sprinkle in, and mix well after each addition, the turmeric, tomato, green chilli and salt. Blend in 170–240 ml/6–8 fl oz of water and leave the mixture to cook over a low heat until it begins to bubble.

4 Add half the coriander leaves, stir and cook for another half a minute. Garnish the dish with the remaining coriander leaves.

Exotic herbs and spices are a colourful and common sight in towns across India. The chief skill in their use lies in the subtle blending of fiery spices to enhance rather than overwhelm the flavour of the dish.

MUTTER MUSHROOM BHAJI
Peas and Mushroom Bhaji
SERVES 4

INGREDIENTS

400 g/14 oz button mushrooms

50 g/2 oz onion, finely sliced

2 tbsp oil

¼ tsp cumin seeds, crushed

¼ tsp mustard seeds

100 g/¼ lb tomatoes, chopped

1 green chilli, very finely chopped

150 g/5 oz frozen peas

½ tsp chilli powder

¼ tsp turmeric

½ tsp salt

100 g/¼ lb red peppers, chopped

4 fat cloves garlic, crushed

2 tbsp coriander leaves

chopped spring onion or chives, to garnish

FOOD VALUE

	TOTAL	PER PORTION (¼)
TOTAL FAT	26.9 g	6.7 g
SATURATED FAT	3.6 g	0.9 g
CHOLESTEROL	0	0
ENERGY (kcals/kj)	425/1762	106/441

METHOD

1 Wipe mushrooms clean, slice off the stalks and cut the small mushrooms into halves and the large ones into quarters.

2 Fry the onions gently in the oil and, as they begin to turn a bit pulpy, add the cumin and mustard seeds. Fry for another couple of minutes.

3 Add the tomato and green chilli, followed by the mushrooms and peas. Stir and cook them for a couple of minutes over a medium heat.

4 Add the chilli powder, turmeric and salt, mixing them in well, and cook, uncovered for 5–7 minutes.

5 Finally, stir in the red pepper, garlic and coriander leaves and cook for another 5 minutes until the mixture is quite dry. Garnish with the chopped spring onion or chives.

DUM GOBHI
Cauliflower Steamed with Herbs and Spices

SERVES 4

INGREDIENTS

450 g/1 lb cauliflower

½ tsp chilli powder

¼ tsp turmeric

2 tsp grated ginger

75 g/3 oz tomatoes, chopped

1 green chilli, chopped

½–¾ tsp salt

1 tbsp low-fat natural yogurt

2 tbsp oil

2–3 tbsp coriander leaves, chopped

½ tsp Garnishing Garam Masala
(see page 18)

FOOD VALUE

	TOTAL	PER PORTION (¼)
TOTAL FAT	26.7 g	6.7 g
SATURATED FAT	3.9 g	1 g
CHOLESTEROL	2 mg	0.5 mg
ENERGY (kcals/kj)	392/1624	98/406

This is simple but superb and so low in calories. Make it frequently, serving it with other heavier dishes or on its own at the end of a "sinful" day.

METHOD

1 Wash, drain and cut the cauliflower into small, even-sized florets (about 2.5-cm/1-inch), including the stems.

2 Combine the chilli powder and turmeric, ginger, tomato, green chilli and salt with the natural yogurt in a small bowl.

3 Grease the inside of a medium-sized saucepan liberally with the oil. Put the cauliflower into the saucepan, then pour the spice and yogurt mixture over it. Cover the pan tightly and cook over a low heat for 10–15 minutes (the cauliflower will steam cook in the spicy mixture).

4 Stir in half the coriander leaves, increase the heat to medium and cook with the lid off, shaking the pan or stirring gently from time to time, for another 5–6 minutes, driving off the excess moisture.

5 Turn off the heat and sprinkle the Garnishing Garam Masala and the remaining coriander leaves over the top. Give the pan one final shake, making sure that there is no moisture left (cook it for a little longer, uncovered if there is, as a watery Dum Gobhi will not taste right).

PALAK ALOO
Chunks of Potato Cooked with Fresh Spinach
SERVES 4

INGREDIENTS

400 g/14 oz fresh or frozen leaf spinach

225 g/½ lb potatoes

2 tbsp oil

¼ tsp fenugreek seeds

½ tsp cumin seeds

60 g/2½ oz tomato, chopped

¼ tsp turmeric

½ tsp chilli powder

salt to taste

FOOD VALUE

	TOTAL	PER PORTION (¼)
TOTAL FAT	25.9 g	6.5 g
SATURATED FAT	3.1 g	0.8 g
CHOLESTEROL	0	0
ENERGY (kcals/kj)	477/1983	119/496

This is one of my favourite Bhajis, especially if a bunch of fresh fenugreek leaves is added to it. These leaves are called methi and can be obtained from most Asian grocers all year round, but as these shops are not located everywhere, I have left them out of the recipe. If you do find some, just remove the leaves themselves from the hard, stringy stalks and substitute these for 2 oz of the spinach. The leaves are highly aromatic and even this small quantity is enough to infuse the whole dish with its distinct, appetizing flavour.

Measure the fenugreek seeds carefully as any more will give the dish a bitter taste.

METHOD

1 If you are using fresh spinach, weigh it after you have removed the stalks and chopped it. Wash it thoroughly to remove all the hidden grit and leave it to drain in a colander. If you are using frozen spinach, defrost it and let it drain well in a colander.

2 Scrub the potatoes well and do not peel them. Cut the potatoes into quarters, then cut each quarter into 2 or more pieces, making 8 to 12 pieces from each potato.

3 Heat the oil in a medium-sized heavy saucepan and fry the fenugreek and cumin seeds. As the seeds begin to sizzle, add the tomato, turmeric, chilli powder and salt. Mix and cook the mixture for half a minute.

4 Add the spinach and potato and mix well so that the vegetables become well coated in the spices.

5 Cover the pan and simmer for 15–20 minutes. If there is still a little moisture left after this time, remove the lid and dry it out a little by cooking rapidly over a medium to high heat for another few minutes, taking great care not to let it burn.

Lentils & Beans

Butter Turka Daal

SERVES 4

INGREDIENTS

175 g/6 oz red lentils
2 tsp Ginger and Garlic Paste (see page 17)
pinch of turmeric
1 green chilli, chopped
½ tsp salt
15 g/½ oz butter
2–3 cloves garlic, chopped
2–3 whole dried chillies
½ tsp cumin seeds
¼ tsp Garnishing Garam Masala (see page 18)
1 tbsp chopped chives

FOOD VALUE

	TOTAL	PER PORTION (¼)
TOTAL FAT	14.3 g	3.6 g
SATURATED FAT	8.4 g	2.1 g
CHOLESTEROL	35 mg	9 mg
ENERGY (kcals/kj)	588/2485	147/621

When served with rice, this meal is known as Dal Bhaat in India and Dal Chaval in Pakistan and is one of the most popular meals in both countries. In the UK it is generally called Turka Daal. Rice and lentils is an old, traditional combination and an all-time favourite. The poor eat it because it is what they can afford, and the rich eat it because they happen to like the taste.

Do not be worried about the use of the whole dried chillies. When you are ready to serve, you can pick them out and use them for garnishing so that you will not bite into them by mistake. They are worth trying as they lend the dish their own subtle flavour which cannot be achieved by using chilli powder. If you do use chilli powder instead, add it with the Ginger and Garlic Paste. *Never* use chilli powder in the Turka process, step 4, as it will burn and spoil the taste and colour of the dish.

METHOD

1 The red lentils can be cooked without pre-soaking them, just put them into a medium-sized heavy saucepan, wash them in 2–3 changes of water, then drain them.

2 Add 570 ml/1 pint of water, the Ginger and Garlic Paste, turmeric, green chilli and salt. Bring to the boil gradually over a medium heat, then lower the heat, cover, and simmer for 30 minutes.

3 Stir vigorously with a wooden spoon to help break up the lentils. Cook for about 10 more minutes until the lentils have become soft and mushy – an indication that they are cooked and ready for the Turka, the tempering of the dish, which you do next as follows.

4 Melt the butter in a small frying pan over a low heat. Add the garlic, whole dried chillies and cumin seeds to the pan.

5 As soon as the seeds begin to sizzle, the chillies turn a shade darker and the garlic pieces become pale pink, which will take about 2 minutes, pour the butter mixture over the lentils. Stir it well and simmer for another 2–3 minutes. Sprinkle the Garnishing Garam Masala and chives over the top just before serving. Take out the whole chillies before serving if you wish.

MALIKA MASOOR DAAL
Whole Brown Lentils
SERVES 4

INGREDIENTS

| 175 g/6 oz brown lentils |
| 2 tsp grated ginger |
| a pinch turmeric |
| ½ tsp salt |
| 15 g/½ oz butter |
| 25 g/1 oz onion, chopped |
| 3–4 cloves garlic, chopped |
| ½ tsp cumin seeds |
| 2–3 whole dried chillies (optional) and ½ tsp chilli powder |
| 1–2 tbsp coriander leaves, chopped |

FOOD VALUE

	TOTAL	PER PORTION (¼)
TOTAL FAT	15.7 g	3.9 g
SATURATED FAT	8.5 g	2.1 g
CHOLESTEROL	35 mg	9 mg
ENERGY (kcals/kj)	640/2704	160/676

The word Malika means the Queen, and the humble brown lentil has been honoured with this name because it is so popular. Underneath those turtle-brown shells lie the split red lentils that are more commonly seen in the West. Though the cooking methods for both lentils are somewhat similar, the taste and the look of the dish will vary a great deal. The brown lentil has an earthy taste of its own and makes a soft, brown, thick, soupy sauce.

METHOD

1 Pick over the lentils (if you need to), then pour them into a medium-sized heavy saucepan, wash them in a few changes of water, then soak them in 714 ml/1¼ pints of water for 30 minutes.

2 Add the ginger, chilli powder, turmeric and salt and bring to a rapid boil. Reduce the heat and simmer for 30 minutes.

3 Although the lentils will be tender and soft at this stage, they will still have that insipid, watery look about them. Continue cooking and, at the same time, try to break or mash some of the lentils against the side of the saucepan with the back of a wooden spoon until the mixture takes on a

thick, dissolved and mushy look.

4 Melt the butter in a small frying pan, add the onions and fry them until they begin to turn translucent.

5 Add the garlic, cumin seeds and whole dried chillies if using any – it will take about ½ a minute for the garlic to turn pink. Then, add this sizzling mixture to the simmering lentils, stir and leave it to simmer for another few minutes, and serve.

DAAL KE SHAMI KEBABS
Moong Daal Patties
SERVES 4

INGREDIENTS

100 g/¼ lb moong daal
3 cloves
1 black cardamom pod, slit
1.25-cm/½-inch piece cinnamon stick
2 tsp grated ginger
2–3 cloves garlic, peeled
½ tsp chilli powder
½ tsp salt
1 green chilli, chopped
175 g/6 oz mashed potato
½ tsp cumin seeds, crushed
3 tbsp coriander leaves, chopped
2 tsp mint sauce
2 tsp lemon juice
2 spring onions, chopped
2 tsp oil
1 size 4 egg, beaten

FOOD VALUE

	TOTAL	PER PORTION (⅛)
TOTAL FAT	28.5 g	3.5 g
SATURATED FAT	4.4 g	0.5 g
CHOLESTEROL	181 mg	27 mg
ENERGY (kcals/kj)	663/2785	84/348

Moong daal, or mung beans are used here. If you cannot find split moong daal, you could use the whole kind, just soak and cook it a bit longer.

METHOD

1 Wash the moong daal in several changes of water, then soak them in 570 ml/1 pint of water for an hour so that they soften and swell slightly. Then drain them off.

2 Pour 240 ml/8 fl oz of fresh water into a heavy saucepan, together with the cloves, black cardamom, cinnamon stick, ginger, garlic, chilli powder and salt. Cook the moong daal in this spiced water for 25–30 minutes, covered, over a medium heat or until the water disappears completely. To help quicken the evaporation, take the lid off during the last 10 minutes of cooking time. Stir occasionally to make sure it is not sticking to the bottom of the pan.

3 Once the liquid has evaporated, let the moong daal cool and discard the whole spices.

4 Grind the moong daal together with the green chilli, roughly, in a blender.

5 Add the mashed potato, cumin seeds and coriander leaves to the daal mixture and blend them thoroughly.

6 Combine the mint sauce, lemon juice, spring onion and a pinch of salt in a small bowl, then put to one side. Now make the Kebabs. Divide the lentil mixture into 8 equal portions and form each portion into a ball. Make a little dent in the middle and put a little of the onion mixture into it. Cover the filling and flatten the ball into a burger shape.

7 Grease a large, non-stick frying pan with half of the oil and heat it. Dip each Kebab into the beaten egg and fry 4 of them first, gently turning them once only. They should be completely heated through, crispy and golden brown. Use the remaining oil to cook the last 4 in the same way.

Mixed Masala Beans

SERVES 4

INGREDIENTS

1 tbsp oil
50 g/2 oz onion, chopped
½ tsp cumin seeds
½ tsp chilli powder
¼ tsp turmeric
¼ tsp Garam Masala (see page 18)
225 g/½ lb chickpeas, tinned, drained
225 g/½ lb kidney beans, tinned, drained
50 g/2 oz tomatoes, chopped
1–2 green chillies, chopped
4 cloves garlic
1 tsp grated ginger
100 g/¼ lb green peppers, chopped
2 tsp lemon juice
2–3 tbsp coriander leaves, chopped

FOOD VALUE

	TOTAL	PER PORTION (¼)
TOTAL FAT	19.3 g	4.8 g
SATURATED FAT	2.3 g	0.6 g
CHOLESTEROL	0	0
ENERGY (kcals/kj)	616/2596	154/649

Not only do the ingredients blend so well together, they also make a very colourful dish.

METHOD

1 Heat the oil in a medium-sized heavy saucepan, then stir in the onion and cumin seeds and fry them until the onions turn a light gold colour.

2 Add the chilli powder, turmeric and Garam Masala and stir. Add 2 tablespoons of water and cook, stirring continuously for a minute or so.

3 Gently stir in the chickpeas, kidney beans, tomato, green chillies, garlic and ginger. Mix well and stir in 240 ml/8 fl oz of water. Bring to the boil, then reduce the heat and simmer for 15–20 minutes.

4 Add the green pepper and cook for 2–3 minutes more.

5 Stir in the lemon juice and half the coriander leaves. Use the remaining coriander leaves to garnish the dish.

KABLI CHANNA
Chickpeas
SERVES 4

INGREDIENTS
450 g/1 lb chickpeas, dried
½ tsp bicarbonate of soda
1 tsp salt

FOOD VALUE	TOTAL	PER PORTION (¼)
TOTAL FAT	24.3 g	6.1 g
SATURATED FAT	2.3 g	0.6 g
CHOLESTEROL	0	0
ENERGY (kcals/kj)	1440/6098	360/1524

All the various celebrations and tea parties in Asian homes could never be the same without chickpeas. Although the thought of soaking them overnight and the lengthy cooking period is a bit offputting, they are so tasty and good for you that it is all worthwhile. Try the next few recipes and see if you feel the same.

Chickpeas are readily available tinned and only need to be drained before using. They are about 40 calories per 30 g/1 oz. They are convenient to have, but you can easily make large batches and freeze what you do not need straight away.

METHOD

1 Wash the chickpeas and soak them overnight in 1.4 l/2½ pints of water in a medium-sized heavy saucepan.

2 Add the bicarbonate of soda and salt and bring to the boil. Skim off the froth, cover the pan with a well-fitting lid and simmer for 45–55 minutes, or until the chickpeas are absolutely tender yet retain their shape.

A cornucopia of nuts and pulses.

Spicy Chickpea Salad

SERVES 4

INGREDIENTS

285 g/10 oz chickpeas, tinned, drained

½ tsp chilli powder

½ tsp cumin seeds, crushed

¼ tsp freshly ground black pepper

3 tbsp coriander and mint leaves, chopped

1 tsp juliennes of fresh ginger

½ tsp rock salt

225 g/½ lb boiled potatoes, cooled

100 g/¼ lb lettuce

75 g/3 oz onion, cut into thin rings

100 g/¼ lb tomatoes, sliced

100 g/¼ lb cucumber, thinly sliced

100 g/¼ lb radishes

wedges of lemon, to garnish

Tamarind Sauce (see page 16)

FOOD VALUE

	TOTAL	PER PORTION (¼)
TOTAL FAT	9.5 g	2.4 g
SATURATED FAT	1.1 g	0.3 g
CHOLESTEROL	0	0
ENERGY (kcals/kj)	557/2361	139/590

Here tinned chickpeas are used for sheer convenience. The best thing about the chickpeas is that they can be cooked without any oil.

METHOD

1 Put the chickpeas into a plastic container with a lid.

2 Sprinkle the chilli powder, cumin seeds, freshly ground black pepper, half the coriander and mint leaves, ginger and the rock salt on the chickpeas. Close the lid firmly and shake the container vigorously so that the chickpeas become evenly coated with the herbs and spices and are even slightly bruised.

3 Dice the potato neatly or slice them thinly, then add them to the chickpeas, mix them in gently.

4 Make a bed of lettuce on each of 4 plates, spoon the spicy chickpea salad onto the lettuce, scatter the remaining coriander and mint leaves and ginger over the top. Surround with cucumber slices, chunks of radishes and sprinkle with lemon juice. Garnish with the onion and tomato and serve with wedges of lemon and lots of Tamarind Sauce.

Masala Chickpeas in Tamarind Sauce

SERVES 4

INGREDIENTS

50 g/2 oz onion, chopped

¼ tsp turmeric

¼–½ tsp chilli powder

*2 tsp Ginger and Garlic Paste
(see page 17)*

½ tsp rock or ordinary salt

*450 g/1 lb chickpeas, cooked or tinned,
drained*

1 tbsp Tamarind Pulp (see page 16)

1 tsp artificial sugar

1–2 green chillies, chopped

100 g/¼ lb tomatoes, sliced

¼ tsp Garam Masala (see page 18)

½ tsp cumin seeds, crushed

2 spring onions, chopped

2–3 tbsp coriander leaves

2 tsp lemon juice

FOOD VALUE

	TOTAL	PER PORTION (¼)
TOTAL FAT	10.1 g	2.5 g
SATURATED FAT	1 g	0.25 g
CHOLESTEROL	0	0
ENERGY (kcals/kj)	588/2490	147/623

METHOD

1 Put the onion, turmeric, chilli powder, Ginger and Garlic Paste and salt into a saucepan. Add 240 ml/8 fl oz of water, bring to the boil, then reduce the heat and simmer for 5 minutes.

2 Add the chickpeas, Tamarind Pulp, sugar, green chillies, half the tomato, the Garam Masala and cumin seeds. Stir and cook for a few minutes.

3 Add 100–170 ml/4–6 fl oz of water, cover and simmer for 10–15 minutes.

4 In a separate container, mix the spring onion, the rest of the tomato, the coriander leaves and lemon juice. Use this mixture to garnish the chickpea dish and then either serve straight away or cold.

CHANNA SAAG
Broccoli with Chickpeas
SERVES 4

INGREDIENTS

75 g/3 oz onion, sliced
2 tbsp oil
½ tsp cumin seeds
4 cloves garlic, finely chopped
½ tsp chilli powder
¼ tsp turmeric
salt to taste
350 g/¾ lb broccoli, washed and chopped
75 g/3 oz tomato, chopped
225 g/½ lb chickpeas, tinned, drained
2 tsp grated ginger
1 green chilli, chopped
pinch of Garam Masala (see page 18)

FOOD VALUE

	TOTAL	PER PORTION (¼)
TOTAL FAT	32.1 g	8 g
SATURATED FAT	4.1 g	1 g
CHOLESTEROL	0	0
ENERGY (kcals/kj)	613/2559	153/640

METHOD

1 Soften the onion in the oil in a medium-sized heavy saucepan over a gentle heat.

2 Add the cumin seeds and garlic and cook for another minute or so.

3 Add the chilli powder, turmeric and salt and fry these spices well, adding a little water occasionally until the paste darkens slightly, which will take 2–3 minutes.

4 Add the broccoli and tomato, mix them in, cover the pan tightly and simmer gently for 20 minutes.

5 Gently stir in the chickpeas and add the ginger, green chilli and Garam Masala. Simmer for another 8–10 minutes before serving.

RAJMAH AUR IMLI
Kidney Beans in Tamarind Sauce
SERVES 4

INGREDIENTS

1 tbsp oil
50 g/2 oz onion, chopped
½ tsp cumin seeds
1 tsp Ginger and Garlic Paste (see page 17)
½ tsp chilli powder
a pinch turmeric
¼ tsp Garam Masala (see page 18)
¾ tsp salt
450 g/1lb kidney beans, tinned, rinsed and drained
1 tbsp Tamarind Pulp (see page 16), or 2 tbsp lemon juice
1 tsp grated ginger
1–2 green chillies, chopped
2 tbsp coriander leaves or chopped chives, to garnish

FOOD VALUE

	TOTAL	PER PORTION (¼)
TOTAL FAT	14 g	3.5 g
SATURATED FAT	1.9 g	0.5 g
CHOLESTEROL	0	0
ENERGY (kcals/kj)	580/2444	145/611

METHOD

1 Take a medium-sized heavy saucepan and add the oil, onion and cumin seeds and fry them until the onion changes colour.

2 Add the Ginger and Garlic Paste, chilli powder, turmeric, Garam Masala and salt. Fry this mixture well for 1–2 minutes, adding a tiny amount of water, when necessary, to stop sticking or burning. As soon as the masala paste turns a shade darker, add the kidney beans and chopped tomatoes. Stir and cook for 2–3 minutes until the beans have absorbed the flavour of the spices.

3 Pour in 285 ml/½ pint of water, cover the pan and simmer for 10 more minutes.

4 Add the Tamarind Pulp or lemon juice now, if using, together with the ginger and green chillies. Stir and cook for another 2–3 minutes.

5 Now, with a wooden spoon, mash a few beans against the side of the pan to thicken the sauce, then garnish with the coriander leaves or chives.

Fresh vegetables are the essential basics of practically all Indian food.

RAJMAH
Kidney Beans in a Thick, Spicy Sauce
SERVES 4

INGREDIENTS
175 g/6 oz kidney beans, dried
salt to taste
1-cm/½-inch piece of cinnamon stick
2–3 cloves
a pinch Garam Masala (see page 18)
1 tbsp oil
50 g/2 oz onion
5 ml/1 tsp Ginger and Garlic Paste (see page 17)
¼ tsp turmeric
½ tsp chilli powder
½ tsp grated ginger
1–2 green chillies
2 tbsp coriander leaves
2 tsp lemon juice
1 spring onion, chopped

FOOD VALUE	TOTAL	PER PORTION (¼)
TOTAL FAT	13.7 g	3.4 g
SATURATED FAT	1.7 g	0.4 g
CHOLESTEROL	0	0
ENERGY (kcals/kj)	587/2483	147/621

See the information about cooking kidney beans on page 12 before starting this recipe.

METHOD
1 Wash and soak the beans for 3–4 hours in 1.1 1/2 pints of water.
2 Add the salt, the cinnamon stick and cloves, cover and cook over a high heat for 30 minutes. Then reduce the heat and simmer for 40 more minutes.
3 Heat the oil in a small frying pan and fry the onion until it turns golden brown.
4 Add the Ginger and Garlic Paste, turmeric and chilli powder. Cook the paste well, adding a little sprinkling of water at appropriate intervals to stop it from catching or burning and until it darkens slightly (this takes 2–3 minutes). Add this masala paste to the simmering beans and cook for 15 more minutes.
5 Add the grated ginger, green chillies and coriander leaves.
6 The beans will be soft now so take a wooden spoon and mash a few against the side of the pan to thicken the sauce and give an appetizing, smooth, melting look to the beans. Mix the lemon juice with the spring onion and use this to garnish the dish.

Kidney Beans in a Thick, Spicy Sauce.

LOBIA
Black-eyed Beans in Ginger and Tamarind Sauce
SERVES 4

INGREDIENTS

175 g/6 oz black-eyed beans, dried

2 tsp grated ginger

½ tsp chilli powder

¼ tsp turmeric

½ tsp salt

1–2 green chillies (chopped)

*1 tbsp Tamarind Pulp (see page 16)
or low-fat natural yogurt*

1 tbsp oil

100 g/¼ lb onion, sliced

½ tsp cumin seeds

4–5 cloves garlic, chopped

¼ tsp Garam Masala (see page 18)

2–3 tbsp coriander leaves, chopped

FOOD VALUE

	TOTAL	PER PORTION (¼)
TOTAL FAT	14.4 g	3.6 g
SATURATED FAT	2.5 g	0.6 g
CHOLESTEROL	2 mg	0.5 mg
ENERGY (kcals/kj)	707/2991	177/748

METHOD

1 Wash and soak beans for a couple of hours in at least 850 ml/1½ pints of water in a medium-sized heavy saucepan.

2 Bring the beans to the boil over a medium heat, add half the ginger, the chilli powder, turmeric and salt, then reduce the heat, cover the pan and cook slowly for 45–50 minutes.

3 Add the remaining ginger, the green chillies, Tamarind Pulp or yogurt, mix it well and let it simmer for another 10–15 minutes.

4 In the meantime, heat the oil in a small frying pan and fry the onion and, when it is about to colour, add the cumin seeds and garlic. Remove the pan from the heat just as the garlic is turning golden brown.

5 Pour this mixture into the simmering beans, together with the Garam Masala. Stir and cook for another 5 minutes.

6 Just before serving, stir in the coriander leaves and serve hot.

LOBIA SAAG
Black-eyed Beans and Broccoli
SERVES 4

INGREDIENTS

450 g/1 lb broccoli, chopped

50 g/2 oz onion, chopped

2 tbsp oil

½ tsp cumin seeds

75 g/3 oz tomato, chopped

½ tsp chilli powder

1 tbsp low-fat natural yogurt

4–5 cloves garlic, chopped

350 g/¾ lb black-eyed beans, tinned, drained

1 tsp grated ginger

¼ tsp turmeric

a pinch Garam Masala (see page 18)

¾ tsp salt

FOOD VALUE

	TOTAL	PER PORTION (¼)
TOTAL FAT	29.3 g	7.3 g
SATURATED FAT	4.6 g	1.2 g
CHOLESTEROL	2 mg	0.5 mg
ENERGY (kcals/kj)	812/3410	203/853

METHOD

1 Wash and chop the broccoli into small florets, and chop the stalks as well.

2 In a medium-sized heavy saucepan, fry the onion in the oil until it turns translucent, then add the cumin seeds and let them sizzle for half a minute.

3 Add the broccoli and tomato and cook, stirring continuously, for a minute or so.

4 Add the chilli powder, yogurt and garlic, mix them in and cook for 7–8 minutes over a low heat.

5 Add the black-eyed beans, ginger, turmeric, Garam Masala and salt. Mix them in well and cook for 2–3 minutes.

6 Add 120 ml/4 fl oz of water, bring to the boil, then reduce the heat and simmer for 10–15 minutes.

Curried Baked Beans

SERVES 2

INGREDIENTS

50 g/2 oz onion, chopped

½ tsp cumin seeds, crushed

1 tbsp oil

¼ tsp chilli powder

pinch of turmeric

2 cloves garlic or ¼ tsp garlic powder

1–2 green chillies (optional)

350 g/¾ lb baked beans

2 tsp low-fat natural yogurt

pinch Garam Masala (see page 18)

¼ tsp salt

coriander leaves or mint leaves or chives

FOOD VALUE

	TOTAL	PER PORTION (½)
TOTAL FAT	13.5 g	6.8 g
SATURATED FAT	1.9 g	1 g
CHOLESTEROL	1 mg	0.5 mg
ENERGY (kcals/kj)	429/1802	214/901

This is an "emergency curry" for when the urge to eat something spicy catches you unawares and unprepared. There's nothing in the fridge or freezer that can be turned into an instant curry, so you turn to the larder and there you happen to find a couple of tins of baked beans and, hey presto, a few minutes later you are enjoying a hot, spicy curry. My daughter tells me this recipe was very useful to her while away from home at university.

METHOD

1 Fry the onion and cumin seeds in the oil in a saucepan. As soon as the onion turns translucent, add 1 tablespoon of water, then the chilli powder, turmeric, garlic and green chillies, if using.

2 Add another 2 tablespoons of water and cook this mixture for 2–3 minutes.

3 Add the baked beans, yogurt, Garam Masala, salt and stir. Also add 4 tablespoons of hot water, cover and simmer for 2–3 minutes.

4 Stir in the lemon juice, coriander or mint leaves or chives and remove from the heat.

PLAIN STEAMED RICE

LENTIL RICE

MUTTER PILLAU

CHICKPEA AND PEPPER PILLAU

Rice Dishes

PRAWN AND COCONUT PILLAU

CHANNA DAAL KHICHIRI

SUBZI AUR MASALA KHICHIRI

LUSSAN KI KHICHIRI

TAHIRI

SUBZI KI BIRYANI

LAMB OR BEEF BIRYANI

CHANNA DAAL BIRYANI

PRAWN AND MUSHROOM BIRYANI

DAAL AUR JHINGA BIRYANI

Plain Steamed Rice

SERVES 4

INGREDIENTS

200 g/7 oz basmati (or long grain) rice

340 ml/12 fl oz water

FOOD VALUE

	TOTAL	PER PORTION (¼)
TOTAL FAT	1 g	0.25 g
SATURATED FAT	Tr	Tr
CHOLESTEROL	0	0
ENERGY (kcals/kj)	718/3004	180/751

METHOD

1 Wash the rice under running cold water and drain. Put it into a medium-sized heavy saucepan with the measured water and let it soak for 10–15 minutes.

2 Bring it to a rapid boil over a medium heat, then reduce the heat so that the water is barely simmering. Cover the pan with a well-fitting lid that does not let out any steam and leave it to cook for about 15 minutes.

It is important that you suppress any temptation to lift the lid to take a peek during this time as your valuable steam will escape, hindering the process of cooking.

Lentil Rice

SERVES 4

INGREDIENTS

175 g/6 oz basmati (or long grain) rice

30 g/10 oz red lentils

340 ml/12 fl oz water

FOOD VALUE

	TOTAL	PER PORTION (¼)
TOTAL FAT	1.2 g	0.3 g
SATURATED FAT	Tr	Tr
CHOLESTEROL	0	0
ENERGY (kcals/kj)	708/2967	177/742

This is not a traditional lentil and rice Khichiri because it would normally be cooked with fried onions and whole spices.

METHOD

1 Combine the rice with the red lentils, wash them and drain well and put them into a medium-sized heavy saucepan.

2 Pour in the fresh water and soak for 10–15 minutes.

3 Over a medium heat, bring it to the boil, then, straight away, reduce the heat, cover the pan with a well-fitting lid and leave it to simmer gently for about 15 minutes. Do *not* lift the lid during this time.

4 Switch off the heat and leave the pan to stand for 2–3 minutes to let the steam work its final magic.

MUTTER PILLAU
Pillau with Peas
SERVES 4

INGREDIENTS

225 g/½ lb rice
75 g/3 oz onion, sliced
2 tbsp oil
2–3 cloves
1-cm/½-inch piece cinnamon stick
1 brown cardamom pod, slit or bruised
1 tsp cumin seeds
100 g/¼ lb peas, fresh or frozen
1 tsp salt

FOOD VALUE

	TOTAL	PER PORTION (¼)
TOTAL FAT	24.8 g	6.2 g
SATURATED FAT	2.9 g	0.7 g
CHOLESTEROL	0	0
ENERGY (kcals/kj)	1116/4649	279/1162

METHOD

1 Wash and soak the rice for 20 minutes, then drain it well and put it to one side.

2 Fry the onion in the oil in a heavy saucepan. Add the cloves, cinnamon stick, cardamom pod and cook until the onions become a rich brown colour.

3 Add 400 ml/14 fl oz of water and let it come to the boil.

4 Add the rice and peas at this stage, stir in the salt and reduce the heat so it is just simmering. Cover the pan with a well-fitting lid and cook for 20 minutes. Let it stand for 2–3 minutes before serving.

Opposite:
Paddy fields in the south of India.

Chickpea and Pepper Pillau

SERVES 4

INGREDIENTS
200 g/7 oz basmati (or long grain) rice
2 tbsp oil
50 g/2 oz onion
1.25-cm/½-inch piece cinnamon stick
3 cloves
1 black cardamom pod, slit or bruised
2–3 bay leaves
½ tsp cumin seeds
175 g/6 oz chickpeas, cooked or tinned, drained
¾ tsp salt
75 g/3 oz red and green peppers, chopped
3–4 cloves garlic, chopped

FOOD VALUE	TOTAL	PER PORTION (¼)
TOTAL FAT	28.7 g	7.2 g
SATURATED FAT	3.1 g	0.8 g
CHOLESTEROL	0	0
ENERGY (kcals/kj)	1125/4697	281/1174

The mixture of red and green peppers makes this dish wonderfully colourful.

METHOD

1 Wash the rice, then soak it for 15–20 minutes. Drain it well and keep it to one side.

2 Heat the oil in a medium-sized heavy saucepan and fry the onion together with the cinnamon stick, cloves, cardamom pod, bay leaves and cumin seeds until the onion turns a rich golden colour.

3 Add 340 ml/12 fl oz of water and bring it to the boil.

4 As soon as the water begins to bubble, add the rice, chickpeas and salt, cover the pan with a well-fitting lid and simmer for 12–15 minutes.

5 Mix in the peppers and garlic gently with a fork, then cover again and let it steam for another 3–5 minutes. Let is stand for a few minutes before serving.

Prawn and Coconut Pillau

SERVES 4

INGREDIENTS
75 g/3 oz onion
2 tbsp oil
1 tsp cumin seeds
3 cloves
1.25cm/½-inch piece cinnamon stick
1 black cardamom pod, slit or bruised
3 cloves garlic, chopped
1 tsp grated ginger
1 tbsp desiccated coconut
½ tsp salt
175 g/6 oz prawns
1 tbsp low-fat natural yogurt
225 g/½ lb basmati (or long grain) rice

FOOD VALUE	TOTAL	PER PORTION (¼)
TOTAL FAT	36.2 g	9 g
SATURATED FAT	11.7 g	2.9 g
CHOLESTEROL	144 mg	36 mg
ENERGY (kcals/kj)	1338/5587	335/1397

METHOD

1 Fry the onions in the oil in a medium-sized heavy saucepan, adding the cumin, cloves, cinnamon stick and cardamom pod, cooking until the onion turns a rich golden colour.

2 Add the garlic, ginger, coconut and salt and cook these together for a few seconds.

3 Add the prawns and yogurt, mix well and cook for another minute.

4 Add the rice and stir it in. Pour in 400 ml/14 fl oz of water, cover the pan and simmer for 20 minutes. Let it stand for another 2–3 minutes before serving.

Prawn and Coconut Pillau.

CHANNA DAAL KHICHIRI
Lentils and Rice with Fried Onions
SERVES 4

INGREDIENTS

200 g/7 oz rice
50 g/2 oz channa daal
75 g/3 oz onion, sliced
1 tbsp oil
1 tsp cumin seeds
1-cm/½-inch piece cinnamon stick
2 cloves
1 brown cardamom pod, slit or bruised
10–12 peppercorns (optional)
½ tsp salt

FOOD VALUE

	TOTAL	PER PORTION (¼)
TOTAL FAT	28.5 g	7.1 g
SATURATED FAT	3.4 g	0.9 g
CHOLESTEROL	0	0
ENERGY (kcals/kj)	1173/4909	293/1227

Khichiri is an all-in-one convenient and very popular rice meal in India and Pakistan. The same dish made its name as Kedgeree in the West in the good old Victorian era and, for some reason, it was known as a breakfast dish, with the difference that fish is added to the dish instead of lentils.

Lentils are always an important ingredient of Khichiri – without them this rice dish would be a simple pillau or Bhugarey chavel or, perhaps, plain fried rice.

There are quite a few varieties of Khichiri. Essentially a rice and lentil dish, vegetables are sometimes added.

METHOD

1 Wash the rice and channa daal separately, and then soak them in 570 ml/1 pint of water for 20–25 minutes. Drain them well, then put them to one side.

2 Fry the onions in the oil in a medium-sized heavy saucepan, together with the cumin seeds, cinnamon stick, cloves, cardamom pod and peppercorns until the onions turn a deep, rich golden brown (here the fried onions also act as a dye – the browner the onions, the richer the colour they will turn the rice).

3 Add 510 ml/18 fl oz of water and put in the channa daal first; let it come to a boil, reduce heat to a minimum, and cover and cook for 10 minutes. Add the drained rice, and salt, stirring gently to mix the lentils and rice together. Cover and continue to cook for 20–25 minutes. Let it stand for 3–4 minutes before serving.

Delightful painted patterns and colours are found on many buildings throughout India, and this love of diversity is seen in the country's cuisine, too. The rich variety of life is apparent everywhere.

SUBZI AUR MASALA KHICHIRI
Rice, Lentil and Vegetable Khichiri
SERVES 4

INGREDIENTS

50 g/2 oz red lentils
200 g/7 oz basmati (or long grain) rice
75 g/3 oz onion, chopped
1.25-cm/½-inch piece cinnamon stick
2–3 cloves
1 black cardamom pod, slit or bruised (optional)
1 tsp cumin seeds
2 tbsp oil
¼ tsp turmeric
½ tsp chilli powder
1 tsp salt
2 tsp Ginger and Garlic Paste (see page 17)
1 tbsp low-fat natural yogurt
75 g/3 oz green beans, chopped
75 g/3 oz carrot, diced
50 g/2 oz tomato, chopped

FOOD VALUE

	TOTAL	PER PORTION (¼)
TOTAL FAT	25 g	6.2 g
SATURATED FAT	3.2 g	0.8 g
CHOLESTEROL	2 mg	0.5 mg
ENERGY (kcals/kj)	1182/4943	296/1235

METHOD

1 Wash lentils and rice together, then soak them in 570 ml/1 pint of water for 15–20 minutes. Then drain them well and keep to one side.

2 Fry the onion, cinnamon stick, cloves, cardamom pod, if using, and cumin seeds in the oil in a medium-sized heavy saucepan.

3 As the onion turns a deep golden colour, add the turmeric, chilli powder, salt, Ginger and Garlic Paste and the yogurt and fry this masala mixture, adding a little water at a time for 2–3 minutes.

4 Add the green beans, carrot and tomato, mix and cook for a minute or so. Add the rice and lentil mixture, stir to blend, then add 425 ml/15 fl oz of water, cover the pan with a tight-fitting lid and bring it to the boil. Reduce the heat and simmer for 20 minutes, then let it stand for 3–4 minutes before serving.

substituted eggplant, pepper + zucchini for carrot + beans

LUSSAN KI KHICHIRI
Garlic Khichiri
SERVES 4

INGREDIENTS

50 g/2 oz moong daal
200 g/7 oz basmati (or long grain) rice
6–7 plump cloves garlic, chopped or crushed
2 tbsp chives, chopped
1 tsp lemon juice
2 tbsp oil
75 g/3 oz onion, sliced
1 tbsp yogurt
2–3 cloves
1.25-cm/½-inch piece cinnamon stick
½ tsp cumin seeds
½ tsp salt

FOOD VALUE

	TOTAL	PER PORTION (¼)
TOTAL FAT	24.2 g	6 g
SATURATED FAT	3 g	0.8 g
CHOLESTEROL	2 mg	0.5 mg
ENERGY (kcals/kj)	1130/4723	283/1181

METHOD

1 Wash the moong daal and rice together and soak them for 15–20 minutes. Then drain them well and put them to one side.

2 Mix the garlic with chives and lemon juice in a small bowl and keep this mixture to one side.

3 Heat the oil in a medium-sized heavy saucepan and add the onion, cloves, cinnamon stick and cumin seeds. Fry until the onion is golden and stir in the yogurt.

4 Add 425 ml/15 fl oz of water and the salt. As soon as the water comes to the boil, add the rice and moong daal mixture, reduce the heat, cover with a well-fitting lid and simmer for 10–12 minutes.

5 Make 2–3 deep dents in the surface of the rice with a tablespoon and gently drop the garlic and chive mixture into them, then cover it up with the rice. Cook, covered, for a further 7–8 minutes. Let the dish stand for a few minutes before serving.

TAHIRI
Masala Rice with Potatoes
SERVES 4

INGREDIENTS

225 g / ½ lb potatoes
225 g / ½ lb basmati (or long grain) rice
2 tbsp oil
75 g / 3 oz onion, chopped
2–3 cloves
1.25-cm / ½-inch piece cinnamon stick
1 black cardamom pod, bruised or slit
2–3 bay leaves
½ tsp cumin seeds
2 tsp Ginger and Garlic Paste (see page 17)
¼ tsp turmeric
½ tsp chilli powder
¾ tsp salt
1 tbsp low-fat natural yogurt
1 green chilli, chopped

FOOD VALUE

	TOTAL	PER PORTION (¼)
TOTAL FAT	24.2 g	6.1 g
SATURATED FAT	2.9 g	0.7 g
CHOLESTEROL	2 mg	0.5 mg
ENERGY (kcals/kj)	1230/5139	307/1285

This has been one of my favourite rice dishes ever since my school days. I loved it so much I was convinced I could live on it for the rest of my life! At home we served it with mint and raw mango or fresh coriander and garlic sauce and a special raita made with tiny chickpea flour dumplings and every time I ate it, I thought I was in heaven!

METHOD

1 Scrub the potatoes well, do not peel them, then cut them into eighths.

2 Wash and soak the rice for 10–15 minutes, then drain it well and keep it to one side.

3 Heat the oil in a medium-sized heavy saucepan, add the onion, the cloves, cinnamon stick, cardamom pod and cumin seeds and fry until the onion turns a rich golden colour.

4 Add the Ginger and Garlic Paste, turmeric, chilli powder and salt. Stir and cook the spices well, then add the yogurt and 15 ml/1 tablespoon of water to prevent it sticking and burning.

5 Add 425 ml/15 fl oz of water, let it come to the boil, then add the rice, potatoes and green chilli. Cover the pan tightly and simmer for about 25 minutes. Then let it stand for another 3–4 minutes before serving.

SUBZI KI BIRYANI
Mixed Vegetable Biryani
SERVES 4

INGREDIENTS

225 g/½ lb basmati rice

75 g/3 oz button mushrooms

75 g/3 oz green beans

2 tbsp low-fat natural yogurt

3 tbsp oil

100 g/4 oz onion, chopped

½ tsp Roasted and Crushed Cumin Seeds (see page 17)

¼ tsp black cumin seeds (optional)

3–4 cloves garlic, chopped or crushed

2 tsp grated ginger

¼ tsp turmeric

½ tsp chilli powder

½ tsp salt

75 g/3 oz red peppers, chopped

50 g/2 oz frozen peas

75 g/3 oz tomato, chopped

2 green chillies, chopped

a pinch grated mace

1 tbsp sterilized cream

2 tbsp mint or coriander leaves, chopped

3 cloves

1.25-cm/½-inch piece cinnamon stick

3–4 green cardamom pods, slit

2–3 bay leaves

FOOD VALUE

	TOTAL	PER PORTION (¼)
TOTAL FAT	40 g	10 g
SATURATED FAT	6.6 g	1.6 g
CHOLESTEROL	12 mg	3 mg
ENERGY (kcals/kj)	1334/5550	334/1387

METHOD

1 Wash the rice, soak it for 15–20 minutes, then drain it very well.

2 Wipe the mushrooms clean and slice the large ones into halves or quarters, leaving the tiny ones whole.

3 Wash, top and tail and de-string the beans, then cut them into 1-cm/½-inch lengths.

4 Dilute the yogurt with 45–60 ml/ 3–4 tablespoons of water and keep this mixture to one side.

5 Heat a third of the oil in a medium-sized heavy saucepan and fry the onion and Cumin Seeds together. As soon as the onions turn a golden colour, lift them out and put them in a sieve pressing them with a wooden spoon to squeeze the oil back into the saucepan.

6 Add the remaining oil to the same pan, and as it heats up, add the black cumin seeds, if using, garlic and ginger and let them sizzle for ½ a minute.

7 Add the turmeric, chilli powder and salt. Cook the spices together, stirring continuously for another minute or so.

8 Now add the mushrooms, red peppers, green beans, peas, tomato and green chillies. Stir to mix them in well, then cover the pan and simmer for 8–10 minutes. Increase heat to medium, remove the lid and, stirring occasionally, cook until the moisture has evaporated and the curry appears

to be fairly dry and add the mace. (Too much moisture will run through the rice layers later and will ruin your Biryani.)

9 Spoon in the cream and mint or coriander leaves, reserving some for garnishing, mix gently and remove the pan from the heat.

10 Add the cloves, cinnamon stick, cardamom pods, bay leaves and a pinch of salt to a medium-sized heavy saucepan together with 1.1 l/2 pints of water and bring it to the boil on high heat. As it begins to bubble, add the rice and let it cook in rapidly boiling water for just 2 minutes – be strict about this as the rice must be only par-boiled at this stage. Drain it well and rinse out the pan.

11 Transfer the rice to a large platter, discarding the whole spices. Add the fried onion and cumin mixture to it, mixing gently with a fork, then divide the mixture into three equal piles.

12 Take your cleaned saucepan and spread the first pile of rice evenly over the bottom. Spoon half the vegetable mixture evenly over the bed of rice. Cover the vegetable mixture with the second pile of rice, again spreading it evenly. Repeat the last 2 steps, then garnish the top with the reserved mint or coriander leaves. Pour the diluted yogurt evenly over the rice. Cover the pan with a well-fitting lid and simmer gently for 20–25 minutes, or until the rice is tender.

Lamb or Beef Biryani

SERVES 4

INGREDIENTS

225 g/½ lb basmati rice

225 g/½ lb lean lamb or beef
(leg of lamb or braising steak)

3 tbsp low-fat natural yogurt

½ tsp black cumin seeds (optional)

½ tsp chilli powder

½ tsp Garam Masala (see page 18)

2 tbsp Ginger and Garlic Paste
(see page 17)

1 tsp salt (optional)

¼ tsp saffron

3 tbsp hot skimmed milk

3 tbsp oil

100 g/¼ lb onion, chopped

5 green cardamom pods, bruised or slit

2 black cardamom pods, bruised or slit

4 cloves

2 green chillies, chopped

2 tsp lemon juice

a pinch freshly grated mace

1.25-cm/½-inch piece cinnamon stick

2–3 bay leaves

½ tsp cumin seeds, crushed

2 tbsp coriander leaves

FOOD VALUE

	TOTAL	PER PORTION (¼)
TOTAL FAT	55.3 g	13.8 g
SATURATED FAT	14.2 g	3.5 g
CHOLESTEROL	184 mg	46 mg
ENERGY (kcals/kj)	1590/6630	398/1658

Biryanis are some of the richest and most exotic dishes in the Indian cook's repertoire. Milk, cream, nuts and dry fruits, the inclusion of anything is possible! The following recipes are a few simple, rather innocent versions of this dish – far less sinful calorie-wise, but enormously pleasing in taste and flavour. You will have to agree that,

no matter what, a Biryani is a Biryani and, as such, is unquestionably one of the true queens of all rice dishes.

Biryanis are famous for their richness, but, here, my aim has been to limit the calories to no more than 400. You should not need to add much in terms of accompaniments either so you can save calories here, too. All they need, at the most, is a cool, simple raita, lightly garnished, perhaps, with some crunchy vegetables, or any of the meat, fish or vegetable kebabs.

When serving a Biryani from the saucepan, stab the serving spoon into it, piercing it all the way down to the bottom of the pan so that it cuts through the layers very much like a cake, then lift out all three layers and gently spread the rice, very much like opening a Japanese fan, from the centre to the edge of the serving dish or plate.

I recommend that you use only the basmati rice when making Biryani. If you put the very best of everything you have into this dish you will be richly rewarded.

METHOD

1 Wash the rice, soak for 20–25 minutes, and drain it very well.

2 Wash and cut the lamb or beef into cubes not bigger than 2.5-cm/1-inch.

3 Mix the yogurt with the black cumin seeds, if using, chilli powder, Garam Masala, Ginger and Garlic Paste and salt in a small bowl and marinate the lamb or beef pieces in it.

4 If using saffron, heat a small frying pan. Place the saffron strands in it

and switch the heat off. Move them about with a wooden spoon while the pan is hot, then leave them there to cool. This makes them crispy and easy to crush. Crush them into a powder with the tips of your fingers and add it to the hot, skimmed milk, leaving it to infuse.

5 Heat the oil in a medium-sized heavy saucepan, then add the onion, green and black cardamom pods and cloves. Fry gently until the onion becomes a rich golden brown. Lift most but not all the fried onions, pressing them against the sides of the pan to let as much oil drip back into the pan as possible. Keep these onions to one side.

6 Drop the marinated meat into the same saucepan and stir-fry it quickly, adding about 1 tablespoon of water from time to time, cooking for at least 2–3 minutes over a medium heat.

7 Add the green chillies, lemon juice and mace, reduce the heat, cover with a well-fitting lid and simmer for 15–20 minutes, or until the moisture has been absorbed and the sauce is fairly dry.

8 While the meat is cooking, put the rice into another medium-sized heavy saucepan with 1.1 l/2 pints of water, together with the cinnamon stick, bay leaves and a pinch of salt. It is important at this stage that the rice is only parboiled, so keep a careful eye on it and, once the water begins to bubble rapidly, allow the rice to cook for just 2 minutes, then drain it very well. Rinse out the pan ready for later.

9 Break or crush the reserved fried

onions and mix them with the cumin seeds, then add this mixture to the parboiled rice, mixing it in with a fork, picking out and discarding the whole spices at the same time. Divide the rice into three equal piles on a platter and keep it to one side.

10 Using the same saucepan in which you prepared the rice, spread one of the piles of rice over the bottom of the pan. Spoon half the meat mixture over the rice, spreading it evenly. Dot the top with the coriander leaves. Cover the meat mixture with the second pile of rice. Repeat the last 2 steps again. Finally, pour the saffron milk evenly over the rice, covering its entire surface. Cover the pan with a tight-fitting lid and simmer for 20–25 minutes, or until the rice has cooked through.

Channa Daal Biryani

SERVES 4

INGREDIENTS

225 g/½ lb basmati (or long grain) rice

100 g/¼ lb channa daal

3–4 green cardamom pods, slit or bruised

1 black cardamom pod, slit or bruised

1-cm/½-inch piece cinnamon stick

2–3 bay leaves

1 tsp salt

125 g/5 oz onion, finely sliced

3 tbsp oil

4 cloves

½ tsp cumin seeds

pinch of turmeric

½ tsp chilli powder

¼ tsp Garam Masala (see page 18)

1 tsp Ginger and Garlic Paste (see page 17)

2 tbsp low-fat natural yogurt

pinch of grated nutmeg

2 green chillies, chopped

1 tsp grated ginger

4 tbsp coriander leaves, chopped

2 tsp lemon juice

mint, to garnish

FOOD VALUE

	TOTAL	PER PORTION (¼)
TOTAL FAT	41.7 g	10.4 g
SATURATED FAT	6.1 g	1.5 g
CHOLESTEROL	11 mg	3 mg
ENERGY (kcals/kj)	1579/6602	395/1651

I have used channa daal for this Biryani as it is wholesome and grainy, lending a lovely texture to this dish.

METHOD

1 Wash the rice and channa daal separately and soak each for 20–25 minutes. Then, drain them very well and keep them to one side.

2 Add the green and black cardamom pods, cinnamon stick, bay leaves and a little salt into 1.1 l/2 pints of water in a medium-sized heavy saucepan and bring to the boil, gradually. Add the rice and parboil by letting it cook in rapidly boiling water for just 2 minutes. It is important that the rice is not allowed to cook completely at this stage. Drain it off thoroughly and keep it to one side. Rinse out the pan for use later.

3 Fry the onions in the oil over a medium heat until they are a deep golden colour in places. Spoon most of them out, pressing the spoon well against the side of the pan, draining as much oil back into the pan as possible and keep these to one side.

4 To the remaining few onions in the pan, add the cloves and cumin seeds and stir-fry for half a minute.

5 Add the turmeric, chilli powder, Garam Masala, Ginger and Garlic Paste and salt. Fry these spices well, adding a little water, when necessary to stop the mixture sticking, and stirring continuously.

6 Add the channa daal and 285 ml/10 fl oz of hot water, stir, cover and simmer for 25–30 minutes, or until the channa daal is almost cooked.

7 Add the yogurt and nutmeg and cook until the excess moisture has completely evaporated and the channa dal is absolutely tender, but each one retains its shape.

8 Mix in the green chillies, ginger and half the coriander leaves. Mix well and remove pan from heat.

9 Add the reserved fried onions to the parboiled rice (keeping just a few of them to one side to garnish later) mixing them gently into the rice with a fork, picking out the whole spices as you do so.

10 In your rinsed saucepan, spread half the onion rice in an even layer over the bottom. Spread all the lentil mixture evenly over the rice, then sprinkle the remaining coriander leaves over the top, squeeze the lemon juice over the top, then spread the remaining rice mixture over the channa daal and coriander, covering them completely.

11 Garnish the top with the reserved fried onions and the mint or other green herb, if using. Sprinkle 45–60 ml/3–4 tablespoons of hot water (if the lentils are too dry, add a little more liquid) over the rice, cover the pan with a well-fitting lid and simmer gently for 20–25 minutes, or until the rice is cooked.

Prawn and Mushroom Biryani

SERVES 4

INGREDIENTS

225 g/½ lb rice

225 g/½ lb shelled prawns

75 g/3 oz button mushrooms

3 tbsp oil

15 fenugreek seeds

2 tsp Ginger and Garlic Paste
(see page 17)

2 tbsp low-fat natural yogurt

¼ tsp turmeric

a pinch of freshly grated mace

½ tsp chilli powder

1 tsp salt

1 green chilli, chopped

2 tsp lemon juice

3 tbsp coriander leaves, chopped

2 cloves

1-cm/½-inch piece cinnamon stick

2 bay leaves

2–3 green cardamom pods slit or bruised

¼ tsp cumin seeds, crushed

3 tbsp skimmed milk

2 spring onions, chopped

FOOD VALUE

	TOTAL	PER PORTION (¼)
TOTAL FAT	40 g	10 g
SATURATED FAT	5.7 g	1.4 g
CHOLESTEROL	186 mg	47 mg
ENERGY (kcals/kj)	1421/5931	355/1483

METHOD

1 Wash and then soak the rice for 15–20 minutes. Drain it very well and keep it to one side.

2 Wash and pat the prawns dry.

3 Wipe the mushrooms clean.

4 Heat the oil in a medium-sized heavy saucepan, add the fenugreek seeds, stir-fry them for half a minute then add the Ginger and Garlic Paste, yogurt, turmeric, chilli powder and salt. Mix and cook until the spices darken a little (this should take 1–2 minutes), sprinkling a little water over it if need be, to prevent it burning or sticking.

5 Add the prawns and cook them for half a minute.

6 Stir in the mushrooms, green chilli and mace until everything is well mixed together, then cover the pan and let it simmer for 5 minutes.

7 Remove the lid, increase the heat slightly and evaporate the excess moisture, stirring all the time.

8 Add the lemon juice and half the coriander leaves, give the mixture a final stir and then set it to one side.

9 Add the remaining salt and the cloves, cinnamon stick, bay leaves and cardamom pods to 1.1 l/2 pints of water in a medium-sized heavy saucepan and bring it to the boil gradually over a medium heat. As soon as it begins to bubble, add the rice and boil it for just 2 minutes (watch the time carefully as it is important to only cook it partially at this stage), then drain it very well and pick out the whole spices. Mix the remaining coriander leaves and cumin seeds gently into the rice with a fork and spoon it into 3 equal-sized piles on a platter. Rinse out the pan to use next.

10 Swirl the skimmed milk to cover the bottom of the pan. Spread the first pile of rice evenly over the bottom of the pan, then spoon half the prawn and mushroom mixture over the rice to form an even layer. Repeat these last 2 layers and top with the remaining rice. Garnish it with the spring onion and then sprinkle 45–60 ml/3–4 tablespoons of hot water evenly over the top, cover with a well-fitting lid and simmer gently for 20–25 minutes.

DAAL AUR JHINGA BIRYANI
Lentil and Prawn Biryani
SERVES 4

INGREDIENTS

50 g/2 oz brown lentils
200 g/7 oz basmati rice
2 tbsp oil
12 fenugreek seeds
½ tsp cumin seeds
¼ tsp mustard seeds
2 tsp Ginger and Garlic Paste (see page 17)
½ tsp chilli powder
¼ tsp turmeric
½ tsp salt
225 g/½ lb prawns
1 tbsp low-fat natural yogurt
1–2 green chillies
1 tsp grated ginger
2 tsp lemon juice
3–4 green cardamom pods, slit
2–3 bay leaves
3 cloves
1.25-cm/½-inch piece cinnamon stick
1 spring onion, chopped

FOOD VALUE

	TOTAL	PER PORTION (¼)
TOTAL FAT	25.9 g	6.5 g
SATURATED FAT	3.1 g	0.8 g
CHOLESTEROL	352 mg	88 mg
ENERGY (kcals/kj)	1224/5128	306/1282

Brown lentils make the Biryani nicely grainy so it keeps its shape and does not disintegrate. It is delicious and the turtle-coloured grains look exceptionally pretty.

METHOD

1 Wash the lentils and rice separately, soak them in separate containers for 20 minutes, then drain the rice very well.

2 Drain the lentils, then transfer them to a medium-sized heavy saucepan and pour in 170 ml/6 fl oz of fresh water.

3 Heat the oil in a medium-sized heavy saucepan, add the fenugreek, mustard and cumin seeds and let them sizzle for a minute.

4 Add the Ginger and Garlic Paste, chilli powder, turmeric and salt and fry this mixture, stirring, for a good minute until the spices turn a slightly darker shade, adding a sprinkling of water, if necessary, to prevent the paste sticking or burning.

5 Add the prawns, mix them in well, then stir in the yogurt and cook the mixture briefly over a medium heat, then lower the heat, add half the green chillies and cook for another couple of minutes, making sure that the moisture has evaporated.

6 Cook the lentils over a low heat, adding the ginger, remaining green chillies and a pinch of salt, until the moisture has completely evaporated. The lentils should be soft but not mushy; it is important that they should retain their shape. Stir in the lemon juice.

7 Add the cardamom pods, bay leaves, cloves, cinnamon stick and a pinch of salt to 1.1 l/2 pints of water and bring it to the boil. As soon as it bubbles, pour in the rice with a pinch of salt and let it cook for no more than 3–4 minutes (measure the time exactly as it must only cook partially at this stage). Drain well.

8 Combine the lentils with the rice, discarding the spices as you find them. Mix in the coriander leaves gently with a fork (reserving some for garnishing later). Spoon the rice into three equal piles on a large platter or tray and rinse the pan to use next.

9 Spread the first pile of rice mixture evenly over the bottom of the cleaned pan. Spoon half the prawn mixture evenly over the rice, dotting some of the spring onion over it. Repeat these last 2 steps, then spread the remaining rice mixture over the top, garnishing with the coriander leaves or remaining spring onion. Sprinkle 45–60 ml/3–4 tablespoons of hot water evenly over the top, cover with a well-fitting lid and simmer gently for about 20–25 minutes, or until the rice is thoroughly cooked, adding a little more hot water, if it has become too dry and cook for a little longer.

Unday Aur Mutter Ka Salan

Lussen Aur Mirach Ka Omelette

Egg and Potato Omelette

Egg Dishes

Mushroom Masala Omelette

Khagina

Bhindi Unda

UNDAY AUR MUTTER KA SALAN
Egg and Peas Curry
SERVES 4

INGREDIENTS

8 size 6 eggs
2 tbsp oil
50 g/2 oz onion, chopped
¼ tsp cumin seeds
2 tsp Ginger and Garlic Paste (see page 17)
½ tsp chilli powder
¼ tsp turmeric
½ tsp ground coriander
salt to taste
¼ tsp Garam Masala (see page 18)
75 g/3 oz tomato, chopped
100 g/¼ lb peas, fresh or frozen
1 green chilli, slit
2 tbsp coriander leaves

FOOD VALUE

	TOTAL	PER PORTION (¼)
TOTAL FAT	58.3 g	14.6 g
SATURATED FAT	12.9 g	3.2 g
CHOLESTEROL	1232 mg	308 mg
ENERGY (kcals/kj)	783/3244	196/811

METHOD

1 Hard boil the eggs, remove their shells, then keep them to one side.

2 Heat the oil in a medium-sized heavy saucepan and fry the onion and cumin seeds until the onion is light gold in colour.

3 Add the Ginger and Garlic Paste, chilli powder, turmeric, ground coriander, salt and Garam Masala and fry this mixture well for a couple of minutes, adding, whenever needed, 1 tablespoon of water, to prevent it burning or sticking.

4 Add the whole eggs and tomato, stir gently and cook for a minute.

5 Add 285 ml/½ pint of water and let it come to the boil before adding the peas and green chilli. Cook for another 5 minutes.

6 Stir in the coriander leaves and remove the pan from the heat.

LUSSAN AUR MIRACH KA OMELETTE
Chilli and Garlic Omelette
SERVES 2

INGREDIENTS

3 size 3 eggs
1 green chilli, chopped
2–3 garlic cloves, chopped or crushed
50 g/2 oz onion, chopped
1–2 tbsp coriander leaves or chopped fresh chives
good pinch of chilli powder
¼ tsp cumin seeds
salt to taste
2 tbsp skimmed milk
2 tsp oil

FOOD VALUE

	TOTAL	PER PORTION (½)
TOTAL FAT	24.6 g	12.3 g
SATURATED FAT	6 g	3 g
CHOLESTEROL	658 mg	329 mg
ENERGY (kcals/kj)	323/1344	162/672

Even after so many years in this country, we still enjoy a chilli omelette for Sunday brunch. Many of our English friends have tried this (with parathas, pooris or toast) and they love it too.

Even if you can't afford the luxury of a paratha (a fried Indian bread), which, because it is fried, contains quite a few calories, there is nothing to stop you enjoying this omelette with a chapati, pitta bread or toasted brown bread. The best part is that this dish is very quick and easy to prepare.

METHOD

1 Break the eggs into a bowl and whisk until they are slightly frothy.

2 Add the green chilli, garlic, onion, coriander leaves or chives, chilli powder, cumin seeds and salt, together with the milk and whisk a bit more to mix the herbs and spices well together.

3 Grease a non-stick frying pan with the oil and heat it to smoking point.

4 Pour in the egg mixture and reduce the heat. You can then choose to keep the omelette whole, turning it quickly to cook the other side when the first is done, to fold it and divide it into 2 portions or to make scrambled eggs, stirring and breaking the egg mixture while it is cooking. All of these methods are used in our house to please everyone in the family and all taste good.

Egg and Potato Omelette
SERVES 2

INGREDIENTS

3 size 3 eggs
100 g/¼ lb potatoes
2 spring onions
¼ tsp chilli powder
3 cloves garlic, chopped
½ tsp salt
1 tbsp oil
½ tsp grated ginger
¼ tsp cumin seeds, crushed
2 tbsp coriander leaves, chopped

FOOD VALUE

	TOTAL	PER PORTION (½)
TOTAL FAT	30 g	15 g
SATURATED FAT	6.6 g	3.3 g
CHOLESTEROL	658 mg	329 mg
ENERGY (kcals/kj)	434/1810	217/905

METHOD

1 Break the eggs into a bowl and whisk until they are foaming.

2 Scrub the potatoes, leave the skins on, then finely dice or slice them.

3 Wipe and chop the spring onions.

4 Mix the chilli powder, garlic and half the salt into the eggs.

5 Grease a non-stick pan with the oil and fry the ginger and cumin seeds for a minute.

6 Add the potato and stir-fry it for a minute.

7 Add the salt and 2 tablespoons of water, cover and cook over a low heat for 6–7 minutes, or until the potatoes are almost done, adding a little more water, if need be.

8 Scatter the coriander leaves over the potato mixture and do not stir. Immediately, pour in the egg mixture. Cook until it is firm, finish it under a hot grill. Serve immediately.

Mushroom Masala Omelette

SERVES 2

INGREDIENTS

3 size 3 eggs
1 tsp plain flour
25 g/1 oz green or red pepper, chopped
50 g/2 oz button mushrooms, chopped
1 green chilli, finely chopped
50 g/2 oz onion, thinly sliced
½ tsp chilli powder
¼ tsp garlic powder
1–2 tbsp coriander leaves, chopped
¼ tsp cumin seeds
¼ tsp salt
1 tbsp oil

FOOD VALUE

	TOTAL	PER PORTION (½)
TOTAL FAT	30 g	15 g
SATURATED FAT	6.7 g	3.3 g
CHOLESTEROL	658 mg	329 mg
ENERGY (kcals/kj)	378/1571	189/786

METHOD

1 Separate the eggs, keeping the whites and yolks in separate containers and whisking each.

2 Fold the flour into the egg yolks, together with the pepper, mushrooms, green chilli, onion and all the herbs and spices.

3 Mix the egg whites into the egg yolk mixture and whisk once again, gradually adding 30 ml/2 tablespoons of water.

4 Grease a large, non-stick frying pan with the oil and heat it to smoking point.

5 Straight away, pour in the egg and vegetable mixture, reduce the heat and cook for a minute or so, shaking the pan. Then remove the pan to a hot grill to finish cooking the omelette.

KHAGINA
A Light, Spicy Egg Dish
SERVES 2

INGREDIENTS

50 g/2 oz onion, thinly sliced

2 green chillies, chopped

15 g/½ oz butter

25 g/1 oz red pepper, cut into juliennes

2 cloves garlic

pinch of chilli powder

pinch of salt

2 size 3 eggs

freshly ground black pepper

2 tbsp chives, chopped

FOOD VALUE

	TOTAL	PER PORTION (½)
TOTAL FAT	24.8 g	12.4 g
SATURATED FAT	11.6 g	5.8 g
CHOLESTEROL	474 mg	237 mg
ENERGY (kcals/kj)	305/1262	153/631

This dish can be made in various ways. The very word Khagina brings back a host of wonderful memories of family get-togethers over the weekends, staying up late on Saturday nights and waking up late, starving, wanting a Khagina brunch.

My husband's version is the best and he loves to watch his family fighting over it!

METHOD

1 Sweat the onion and green chillies in the butter in a non-stick frying pan over a low heat for 4–5 minutes, adding a tiny amount of water between stirs to keep them from sticking and burning.

2 Add the red pepper and garlic and cook for 3–4 minutes, stirring continuously.

3 Add the chilli powder, salt and 30 ml/2 tablespoons of water and let it simmer again for 2–3 minutes.

4 Break the eggs gently on top of the bed of vegetables and spices in the pan, taking care to keep the egg yolks intact. Shake the pan so that the egg white spreads to fill the pan. Do not overcook the egg yolks – they are done when, if you were to pierce them with a fork, they would ooze out and run slightly.

5 Grind black pepper over the top, then sprinkle the chives over and serve immediately.

BHINDI UNDA
Egg and Okra Scramble
SERVES 2

INGREDIENTS

100 g/¼ lb okra
1 tbsp oil
50 g/2 oz onion, chopped
¼ tsp cumin seeds
50 g/2 oz tomato, chopped
pinch of turmeric
¼ tsp chilli powder
½ tsp salt
freshly ground black pepper to taste
2 tsp lemon juice
3 size 3 eggs
3 cloves garlic, chopped
1 spring onion, finely chopped

FOOD VALUE

	TOTAL	PER PORTION (½)
TOTAL FAT	31 g	15.5 g
SATURATED FAT	7 g	3.5 g
CHOLESTEROL	658 mg	329 mg
ENERGY (kcals/kj)	407/1694	203/847

METHOD

1 Wash and dry the okra well. Top and tail each one then cut it into 3–4 slices.

2 Heat the oil in a medium-sized non-stick frying pan with a lid. Soften the onion, then add the cumin seeds.

3 Add the okra, tomato, turmeric, chilli powder and half the salt. Stir, then let the vegetables cook in their own moisture by covering the pan with its lid, over a low heat for 10–12 minutes (the okra should then be tender). Mill some black pepper over and sprinkle in the lemon juice.

4 Break the eggs into a bowl and whisk with 2 tablespoons of water. Stir in the garlic, spring onion and the remaining salt.

5 Pour the egg mixture over the vegetable mixture in the pan and, as soon as the eggs are lightly set, break up the mixture and continue to stir while it cooks. Serve immediately.

TORI RAITA

CUCUMBER AND TOMATO RELISH

SPINACH AND TOMATO RAITA

Raita

PIAZ AUR KUKRI KA RAITA

BANGON KA RAITA

All raitas make perfect salad dressings or fillings for jacket potatoes, as well as serving their usual role, tasty relishes to eat with the main course. Even if you cannot afford to have a full portion calorie-wise, just a couple of spoonfuls will make a big difference, enriching any meal.

There are thousands of variations that can be made on the simple basic formula of yogurt and vegetables, so try the following recipes and then let your imagination flow.

TORI RAITA
Courgette and Tomato Raita

SERVES 4

INGREDIENTS

100 g/¼ lb baby courgettes

2 cloves garlic, crushed

pinch of freshly ground black pepper

½ tsp sugar

pinch of salt

225 g/8 oz low-fat natural yogurt

2 tsp mint leaves or mint sauce

pinch of chilli powder

½ tsp cumin seeds, crushed

50 g/2 oz tomato, sliced

FOOD VALUE

	TOTAL	PER PORTION (¼)
TOTAL FAT	2.4 g	0.6 g
SATURATED FAT	1.25 g	0.3 g
CHOLESTEROL	9 mg	2 mg
ENERGY (kcals/kj)	162/683	40/171

METHOD

1 Wipe the courgettes, do not peel, then slice them thinly.

2 Put them into a pan with 4 tablespoons of slightly salted water, cover the pan and simmer for a few minutes until the water has disappeared. Leave to cool, then mash the courgettes roughly until the last of the moisture has been absorbed.

3 Stir the crushed garlic, freshly ground black pepper to taste, the sugar and salt into the mashed courgettes and mix together.

4 Whisk the yogurt lightly until it is smooth, then pour it over the courgette mixture.

5 Stir in the mint or mint sauce, mixing it in gently together with the yogurt.

6 Garnish the dish by "drawing" a red, brown and black circle when you sprinkle on the chilli powder, cumin seeds and black pepper. Use the tomatoes to garnish.

Opposite:
Courgette and Tomato Raita.

Cucumber and Tomato Relish

SERVES 4

INGREDIENTS

225 g/8 oz cucumber

2 tbsp fresh coriander or mint, chopped

115 g/4 oz onion, chopped

1 tbsp vinegar or lemon juice

1 tsp sweetened mint sauce

salt and freshly ground black pepper, to taste

FOOD VALUE

	TOTAL	PER PORTION (¼)
TOTAL FAT	0.4 g	0.1 g
SATURATED FAT	Tr	Tr
CHOLESTEROL	0	0
ENERGY (kcals/kj)	73/303	18/76

METHOD

1 Cut all the vegetables into either cubes or small chunks.

2 Combine the vinegar or lemon juice, mint sauce and salt and pepper.

3 Add the mint or coriander leaves and blend all the ingredients well together. Serve chilled.

Spinach and Tomato Raita

SERVES 4

INGREDIENTS

50 g/2 oz fresh spinach, chopped

225 g/8 oz low-fat natural yogurt

pinch of chilli powder

½ tsp sugar

salt and freshly ground black pepper

2 tsp oil

¼ tsp cumin seeds

¼ tsp mustard seeds (optional)

1 fat clove garlic, chopped

½ tsp grated ginger

50 g/2 oz tomato, sliced

FOOD VALUE

	TOTAL	PER PORTION (¼)
TOTAL FAT	8.6 g	2.1 g
SATURATED FAT	1.9 g	0.5 g
CHOLESTEROL	9 mg	2 mg
ENERGY (kcals/kj)	216/908	54/227

If you decide to substitute frozen for fresh spinach, make sure it is leaf rather than puréed spinach.

METHOD

1 Wash fresh spinach thoroughly, remove the tough stalks, then chop the leaves into thin strips and drain it well. For frozen spinach, drain it well then chop into strips as for fresh.

2 Put the spinach into a small saucepan, cover with a well-fitting lid and cook it in its own moisture over a low heat, briefly, or until it is tender. Leave it to cool.

3 Whisk the yogurt lightly in a medium-sized bowl until it is smooth and add the spinach to it. Blend in the chilli powder, sugar, salt and pepper.

4 Heat the oil in a small frying pan and fry the cumin and mustard seeds, if using, garlic and ginger until the seeds begin to pop (1–2 minutes).

5 Pour this mixture into the yogurt and spinach mixture and mix again. Garnish with the tomato and chill before serving.

PIAZ AUR KUKRI KA RAITA

Spring Onion and Cucumber Raita

SERVES 4

INGREDIENTS

225 g/8 oz low-fat natural yogurt

2–3 tbsp skimmed milk

100 g/¼ lb cucumber, diced

2 spring onions, chopped

½ tsp sugar

salt to taste

¼ tsp Roasted and Crushed Cumin Seeds (see page 17)

pinch of chilli powder

freshly ground black pepper

FOOD VALUE

	TOTAL	PER PORTION (¼)
TOTAL FAT	2.1 g	0.5 g
SATURATED FAT	1.1 g	0.3 g
CHOLESTEROL	9 mg	2 mg
ENERGY (kcals/kj)	155/652	39/163

A quick, everyday kind of raita that can be served with almost any meal.

METHOD

1 Whisk the yogurt and milk lightly together in a bowl until smooth.

2 Add the cucumber, spring onions, sugar, salt and half the Cumin Seeds and mix them in well.

3 Sprinkle the chilli powder over the surface of the raita in a circle, then "draw" an inner circle in the same way with the black pepper and sprinkle the remaining Cumin Seeds in the centre. Alternatively, create your own patterns with these red brown and black colours.

Opposite:
Spring Onion and Cucumber Raita.

BANGON KA RAITA
Aubergine Raita with Sunflower Seeds
SERVES 4

INGREDIENTS

15 g/½ oz sunflower seeds

100 g/¼ lb aubergines, roughly grated

2–3 garlic cloves, crushed

pinch of salt

3–4 tbsp skimmed milk

225 g/8 oz low-fat natural yogurt

1 tsp artificial sugar

¼ tsp cumin seeds, crushed

¼ tsp freshly ground black pepper

75 g/3 oz tomato, chopped

few mint leaves or pinch of dried mint

pinch of chilli powder

FOOD VALUE

	TOTAL	PER PORTION (¼)
TOTAL FAT	9.6 g	2.4 g
SATURATED FAT	2.1 g	0.5 g
CHOLESTEROL	11 mg	3 mg
ENERGY (kcals/kj)	267/1124	67/281

METHOD

1 Put the sunflower seeds into a heavy frying pan and heat it over a medium heat. Move the seeds around continuously with a wooden spoon, roasting them for a minute. Switch the heat off, but keep on shifting the seeds as the pan cools, then leave them there to cool completely.

2 Pour 4 tablespoons of water into a small saucepan, together with the aubergine, garlic and a pinch of salt, then bring it to the boil. Cook for 3–4 minutes until the aubergines have softened to a pulp, then remove the pan from the heat and leave it to one side to cool.

3 Whisk the milk and yogurt together in a bowl until smooth, then add the aubergine, sugar, cumin seeds and pepper and blend well.

4 Add the tomato and mint leaves or dried mint.

5 Sprinkle the chilli powder over the top and garnish with the sunflower seeds just before serving.

Sweets & Drinks

It is a sad fact of life that most Indian sweets are incredibly high in calories. Unlike Western sweets, however, these enormously rich and sugary sweets symbolize festivity and jubilation and so are not eaten every day but just on special occasions.

In Asian homes we generally finish our meals with a bowl of fresh fruit as all kinds of wonderful fruits are abundant at home. Besides enjoying the fruits, the family chatter away and laugh together or discuss serious issues and so this course usually lasts much longer than the main course.

Mango Malai
SERVES 4

INGREDIENTS

225 g/½ lb fresh mango*, flesh only

225 g/½ lb low-fat natural yogurt

2–3 tbsp artificial sugar

2 tsp lemon juice

pinch of nutmeg

pinch of salt

50 g/2 oz black grapes

FOOD VALUE

	TOTAL	PER PORTION (¼)
TOTAL FAT	2.4 g	0.6 g
SATURATED FAT	1.3 g	0.3 g
CHOLESTEROL	9 mg	2 mg
ENERGY (kcals/kj)	284/1210	71/303

Mango Malai is one of my favourite inventions and, if the sheer delight on the faces of my guests is anything to go by, generally extremely popular. There is a similar sweet called Aamruss, which, literally, means the mango juice, but freshly fried, delicate and light pooris are served with it which makes it less of a dessert and more like a first course.

My recipe for Mango Malai is a *bit* wicked: I use a good helping of double cream in it, thus the word Malai in its name, which means cream, but in trying to mend my ways, I have substituted low-fat yogurt and it is still a wonderfully refreshing dessert which has fewer calories!

METHOD

1 Put the mango, yogurt, sugar, lemon juice, nutmeg and salt into a blender and process it until it is smooth.

2 Spoon the mixture into 4 serving dishes. Halve the grapes, discarding the pips, if any, and decorate the dessert with them. Serve chilled.

*If you choose to use tinned mango instead, the finished desserts will contain 40 more calories, or, 10 more calories per portion.

AMROOD-AFZA
Guava and Cottage Cheese Blend
SERVES 4

INGREDIENTS

225 g/½ lb cottage cheese
1 tbsp lemon juice
4 tbsp artificial sugar
2 tsp rosewater (optional)
2 tbsp skimmed milk
225 g/½ lb guavas, tinned
75 g/3 oz fresh plums, sliced

FOOD VALUE

	TOTAL	PER PORTION (¼)
TOTAL FAT	9 g	2.2 g
SATURATED FAT	5.4 g	1.3 g
CHOLESTEROL	29 mg	7 mg
ENERGY (kcals/kj)	383/1626	96/407

METHOD

1 Put the cottage cheese, lemon juice, sugar, rosewater, if using, and milk into a blender and process until smooth.

2 Purée the guavas, together with their seeds and juices.

3 Layer the puréed guavas and cottage cheese mixtures alternately in 4 serving dishes and garnish them with the slices of plum. Serve them chilled.

Indians love sweet things. Here gur *or* jaggery, *a sweet popular with villagers, is a cheap derivative of sugar cane or palm sap, and makes a form of candy.*

Fruit Chaat

SERVES 4

175 g/6 oz guavas, tinned, drained

175 g/6 oz honeydew melon

100 g/¼ lb pears

100 g/¼ lb apple

100 g/¼ lb tangerines

¼ tsp cumin seeds, crushed

pinch of chilli powder

pinch of freshly ground black pepper

pinch of salt

2–3 tsp artificial sugar

2 tbsp fresh orange juice

2 tsp lemon juice

*fresh mint leaves, slightly crushed or
broken, to garnish*

FOOD VALUE

	TOTAL	PER PORTION (¼)
TOTAL FAT	1.3 g	0.3 g
SATURATED FAT	0	0
CHOLESTEROL	0	0
ENERGY (kcals/kj)	210/891	53/223

I am sure you will be surprised to read the list of ingredients: chilli powder and salt and pepper with fruit, in a dessert? Be surprised again when you've tried it and seen for yourself how well it works.

Fruit chaats are very popular at tea parties, dinner parties and other special occasions. They are mostly made using tropical fruits and, as the fresh ones are not always available or of the best quality, I suggest you rely on the tinned ones, choosing those in their natural juices rather than syrup, and just weigh the flesh.

METHOD

1 Cut up all the fruits into small cubes or tiny segments so that the spices can mingle into the fruits easily.

2 Mix all the spices together in a bowl, pour in the sugar, orange and lemon juice, stir and shake the mixture to blend them. Pour this over the fruit, mix gently, garnish with the mint leaves and chill well before serving.

Fruit and Yogurt Chaat

SERVES 4

INGREDIENTS

100 g/¼ lb guavas, tinned, drained
100 g/¼ lb pineapple, tinned, drained
1 banana
225 g/½ lb low-fat natural yogurt
2–3 tbsp artificial sugar
2 tsp lemon juice
pinch of rock salt
pinch of freshly ground black pepper
pinch of cardamom pods, crushed, or pinch of grated nutmeg
50 g/2 oz pomegranate, flesh only or 75 g/3 oz fresh cherries

FOOD VALUE

	TOTAL	PER PORTION (¼)
TOTAL FAT	3 g	0.8 g
SATURATED FAT	1.1 g	0.3 g
CHOLESTEROL	9 mg	2 mg
ENERGY (kcals/kj)	347/1469	87/367

METHOD

1 Cut all the fruit – except the pomegranate – into bite-size pieces.

2 Whisk the yogurt briefly until it is smooth.

3 Add the sugar, lemon juice, salt, pepper and cardamom or nutmeg to the yogurt and mix them together well.

4 Add the fruit to the yogurt and mix them in gently. Divide the mixture between 4 serving dishes. Scatter the pomegranate like pearls over each dish and chill well before serving.

Fruits and fruit juices are the perfect companions to spicy Indian food.

Tropical Fruit Salad

SERVES 4

INGREDIENTS

225 g/½ lb mango flesh

175 g/6 oz honeydew melon

100 g/¼ lb kiwi fruit

125 g/5 oz lychees, tinned

2 tbsp orange juice

2 tsp lemon juice

1 tbsp artificial sugar

FOOD VALUE

	TOTAL	PER PORTION (¼)
TOTAL FAT	1.2 g	0.3 g
SATURATED FAT	0.3 g	Tr
CHOLESTEROL	0	0
ENERGY (kcals/kj)	373/1596	93/399

METHOD

1 Cut the mango into bite-size cubes.

2 Use a melon baller to cut out as many little balls as possible from the melon.

3 Peel and slice the kiwi fruit.

4 Drain the lychees.

5 Mix the orange and lemon juices and sugar together and pour this over the fruit. Mix well and chill.

6 Just before serving, divide the fruit between 4 serving dishes and top each one with whole lychees.

NIMBOO PAANI
Lemon Drink
SERVES 1

INGREDIENTS

juice of half a lemon

275 ml/10 fl oz water

2–3 tbsp artificial sugar

ice cubes as required

fresh mint leaves and lemon wedges to garnish

The literal translation is "lemon water" and it is an equally popular drink in both India and Pakistan. It is made in more or less the same way in Pakistan but goes under the name of Skunjbeen.

No cooking is involved – it is simply made from fresh lemon juice and sugar. If you replace the real sugar with artificial sugar you have "Diet Nimboo Paani" in a matter of minutes. The best part is that you could drink gallons of it without consuming a single calorie. Also, if you drink it during or after a meal it is doubly beneficial – it helps you to enjoy the meal and, at the same time, takes away the urge for a sweet. Drink it between meals if you are feeling peckish for no reason and it will melt your hunger away as well as giving you plenty of Vitamin C.

METHOD

1 Put all but the garnishing ingredients into a blender and blend for a few seconds.

2 Pour into a tall glass and garnish with the mint leaves and lemon wedges.

LASSI
Yogurt Drink
SERVES 2

INGREDIENTS

8 tbsp low-fat natural yogurt

570 ml/1 pint water

2–3 tbsp artificial sugar

ice cubes as required

pinch of salt

4 mint leaves to garnish (optional)

FOOD VALUE

	TOTAL	PER PORTION (½)
TOTAL FAT	3.2 g	1.6 g
SATURATED FAT	2 g	1 g
CHOLESTEROL	16 mg	8 mg
ENERGY (kcals/kj)	224/944	112/472

A delicious, cooling and most satisfying drink. Once you try it, you can easily get hooked on it and, in hot weather, it is almost like an answer to one's prayer! Nothing else quenches your thirst quite the way lassi does.

A small glass of sweet lassi can be served as a liquid dessert, especially following a spicy meal.

Lassi does not necessarily have to be sweet; savoury versions are also very popular – try one with a pinch of salt and leave the sugar out, freshly ground black pepper and chopped mint leaves for slightly spicy taste. Try them and see which one is for you.

METHOD

1 Put all the ingredients, except the mint leaves, into a blender (or use a hand whisk) and blend thoroughly until it becomes frothy.

2 Pour it into a tall glass and add some more ice cubes if you wish. Garnish with the mint leaves, if using, and serve immediately. (If you leave it undrunk for too long, the yogurt separates and rises to the surface, leaving the water underneath it, but all you have to do is just stir it to amalgamate them once more.)

Strawberry Lassi
SERVES 1

INGREDIENTS

50 g/2 oz low-fat natural yogurt

75 g/3 oz fresh or frozen strawberries

1–2 tbsp artificial sugar

ice cubes as required

425 ml/15 fl oz water

FOOD VALUE

	TOTAL	PER SERVING
TOTAL FAT	0.5 g	0.5 g
SATURATED FAT	0.25 g	0.25 g
CHOLESTEROL	2 mg	2 mg
ENERGY (kcals/kj)	48/202	48/202

METHOD

1 Put all the ingredients in a blender and blend for half a minute.

2 Pour into a tall glass, adding more ice cubes if you like.

Melon and Ginger Lassi

SERVES 1

INGREDIENTS

50 g/2 oz low-fat natural yogurt	
75 g/3 oz melon flesh	
½ tsp ground ginger	
1–2 tbsp artificial sugar	
ice cubes as required	
425 ml/15 fl oz water	

FOOD VALUE

	TOTAL	PER SERVING
TOTAL FAT	0.5 g	0.5 g
SATURATED FAT	0.25 g	0.25 g
CHOLESTEROL	2 mg	2 mg
ENERGY (kcals/kj)	42/179	42/179

METHOD

1 Put all the ingredients into a blender and blend until the mixture is frothy.

2 Pour into a tall glass and drop in some more ice if you like.

Index